best of the best
CHICKEN

Publications International, Ltd.
Favorite Brand Name Recipes at www.fbnr.com

Pictured on the front cover: Grilled Chicken with Chimichurri Salsa *(page 83).*
Pictured on the back cover: Chicken and Pasta Salad with Kalamata Olives *(page 116).*

ISBN-13: 978-1-4127-7799-5
ISBN-10: 1-4127-7799-2

Library of Congress Control Number: 2008941506

Manufactured in China.

8 7 6 5 4 3 2 1

Microwave Cooking: Microwave ovens vary in wattage. Use the cooking times as guidelines and check for doneness before adding more time.

Preparation/Cooking Times: Preparation times are based on the approximate amount of time required to assemble the recipe before cooking, baking, chilling or serving. These times include preparation steps such as measuring, chopping and mixing. The fact that some preparations and cooking can be done simultaneously is taken into account. Preparation of optional ingredients and serving suggestions is not included.

contents

wings &things

Tucson Chicken Wings With Blue Cheese Dipping Sauce

3 pounds chicken drummettes or chicken wings, tips removed and cut in half at joint
1 cup LAWRY'S® Mexican Chile & Lime Marinade With Lime Juice
½ cup crumbled blue cheese
¼ cup HELLMANN'S® or BEST FOODS® Real Mayonnaise
¼ cup sour cream

1. In large resealable plastic bag, pour ½ cup LAWRY'S® Mexican Chile & Lime Marinade With Lime Juice over chicken. Close bag and marinate in refrigerator 30 minutes.

2. Meanwhile, in small bowl, combine blue cheese, Mayonnaise, sour cream and 1 tablespoon Marinade; set aside.

3. Remove chicken from Marinade, discarding Marinade. Grill chicken over medium heat, turning frequently and brushing with remaining ½ cup Marinade, 20 minutes until chicken is thoroughly cooked. Serve with Blue Cheese Dipping Sauce.

Note: Also terrific with LAWRY'S® Baja Chipotle Marinade With Lime Juice. *Makes 12 appetizer servings*

Prep Time: 10 minutes
Marinate Time: 30 minutes
Cook Time: 20 minutes

Bacon-Wrapped BBQ Chicken

8 chicken tenders (about 1 pound)
½ teaspoon paprika or cumin (optional)
8 slices bacon
½ cup barbecue sauce, divided

1. Preheat broiler. Line broiler pan with foil; set aside.

2. Sprinkle chicken tenders with paprika, if desired. Wrap each chicken tender with slice of bacon in spiral pattern; place on broiler pan.

3. Broil chicken 4 minutes. Turn and broil 2 minutes. Brush with ¼ cup barbecue sauce; broil 2 minutes. Turn and brush with remaining ¼ cup barbecue sauce. Broil 2 minutes or until chicken is no longer pink in center. *Makes 4 servings*

Almond Chicken Cups

1 tablespoon vegetable oil
½ cup chopped onion
½ cup chopped red bell pepper
2 cups chopped cooked chicken
⅔ cup sweet and sour sauce
½ cup chopped almonds
2 tablespoons soy sauce
6 (6- to 7-inch) flour tortillas

1. Preheat oven to 400°F. Heat oil in small skillet over medium heat. Add onion and bell pepper. Cook and stir 3 minutes or until crisp-tender.

2. Combine vegetable mixture, chicken, sweet and sour sauce, almonds and soy sauce in medium bowl; mix until well blended.

3. Cut each tortilla in half. Place each half in standard (2¾-inch) muffin cup. Fill each with about ¼ cup chicken mixture.

4. Bake 8 to 10 minutes or until tortilla edges are crisp and filling is heated through. Cool on wire rack 5 minutes before serving.
Makes 12 chicken cups

Bacon-Wrapped BBQ Chicken

Lawry's® Grilled Chicken Nachos

¾ cup plus 2 tablespoons LAWRY'S® Herb & Garlic Marinade With Lemon Juice

1 pound boneless, skinless chicken breasts

1 medium onion, cut into ½-inch thick slices

3 medium tomatoes, chopped

1 serrano chili, seeded and finely chopped

½ teaspoon LAWRY'S® Garlic Salt

¼ teaspoon LAWRY'S® Seasoned Pepper

1 bag (11 ounces) plain tortilla chips

2 cups shredded Cheddar or Monterey Jack cheese (about 8 ounces)

1 avocado, diced

1 tablespoon lime juice

1. In large resealable plastic bag, pour ½ cup LAWRY'S® Herb & Garlic Marinade With Lemon Juice over chicken and onion; turn to coat. Close bag and marinate in refrigerator 30 minutes.

2. Meanwhile, in medium bowl, combine tomatoes, chili, LAWRY'S® Garlic Salt and LAWRY'S® Seasoned Pepper; set aside.

3. Remove chicken and onion from Marinade, discarding Marinade. Grill chicken and onion, turning once and brushing with additional ¼ cup Marinade, 10 minutes or until chicken is thoroughly cooked and onion is tender. Shred chicken and chop onion.

4. In medium bowl, combine chicken, onion and remaining 2 tablespoons Marinade. In center of double layer (18×18-inch pieces) heavy-duty aluminum foil, arrange tortilla chips, then top with chicken mixture and cheese. Grill 1 minute or until cheese is melted. To serve, top with tomato mixture, drained if desired, avocado and lime juice. *Makes 6 servings*

Prep Time: 30 minutes
Marinate Time: 30 minutes
Cook Time: 15 minutes

Lawry's® Grilled Chicken Nachos

Cranberry-Barbecue Chicken Wings

3 pounds (about 27 wings) chicken wings
Salt and black pepper
1 jar (12 ounces) cranberry-orange relish
½ cup barbecue sauce
2 tablespoons minute tapioca
1 tablespoon prepared mustard

Slow Cooker Directions

1. Preheat broiler. Cut off chicken wing tips; discard. Cut each wing in half at joint. Place chicken on rack in broiler pan; season with salt and pepper.

2. Broil 4 to 5 inches from heat 10 to 12 minutes or until browned, turning once. Transfer chicken to slow cooker.

3. Stir relish, barbecue sauce, tapioca and mustard in small bowl. Pour over chicken. Cover; cook on LOW 4 to 5 hours.

Makes about 16 appetizer servings

Prep Time: 20 minutes
Cook Time: 4 to 5 hours

Cranberry-Barbecue Chicken Wings

Mexican Drumsticks with Ranchero Dipping Sauce

12 chicken drumsticks (about 3 pounds)
1 packet (1.25 ounces) ORTEGA® Taco Seasoning Mix
1 bottle (8 ounces) ORTEGA® Taco Sauce
1 bottle (8 ounces) ranch dressing
1 cup ORTEGA® Original Salsa

Preheat oven to 350°F. Arrange drumsticks on baking pan. Sprinkle seasoning mix over drumsticks, turning to coat both sides.

Bake 45 minutes; turn drumsticks over halfway through to bake evenly. Remove from oven.

Place taco sauce in large mixing bowl. Add drumsticks and toss to coat evenly. Replace on baking sheet; broil 4 minutes on each side or until crisp.

Combine ranch dressing and salsa to make dipping sauce. Serve with warm drumsticks.   *Makes 12 appetizers*

Tip: Experiment with different flavors of ORTEGA taco sauce for a spicier taste. Or try this recipe with chicken wings for a great alternative to traditional hot wings.

Prep Time: 5 minutes
Start to Finish: 1 hour

Mexican Drumsticks with Ranchero Dipping Sauce

Chicken Wraps

½ pound boneless skinless chicken thighs
½ teaspoon Chinese 5-spice powder
½ cup bean sprouts
2 tablespoons minced green onion
2 tablespoons sliced almonds
2 tablespoons soy sauce
4 teaspoons hoisin sauce
1 to 2 teaspoons chili garlic sauce*
4 large lettuce leaves

Chili garlic sauce is available in the Asian food section of most large supermarkets.

1. Preheat oven to 350°F. Place chicken on baking sheet; sprinkle with 5-spice powder. Bake 20 minutes or until chicken is no longer pink in center. Cool.

2. Dice chicken. Place chicken, bean sprouts, green onion, almonds, soy sauce, hoisin sauce and chili garlic sauce in large bowl. Stir until blended. To serve, spoon ⅓ cup chicken mixture onto each lettuce leaf; roll or fold as desired. *Makes 4 servings*

note

Pungent 5-spice powder is very popular in Chinese and other Asian cuisines. It is usually a mixture of cinnamon, cloves, fennel seed, star anise and Szechuan peppercorns or ginger. You can find it in most supermarkets and Asian grocery stores.

Chicken Wrap

Chicken Empanadas

4 ounces cream cheese

2 tablespoons chopped fresh cilantro

2 tablespoons salsa

½ teaspoon salt

½ teaspoon ground cumin

¼ teaspoon garlic powder

1 cup finely chopped cooked chicken

1 package (about 15 ounces) refrigerated pie crusts (2 crusts), at room temperature

1 egg, beaten

Additional salsa (optional)

1. Heat cream cheese in small heavy saucepan over low heat, stirring constantly, until melted. Add cilantro, salsa, salt, cumin and garlic powder; stir until smooth. Stir in chicken; remove from heat.

2. Roll out pie crust dough on lightly floured surface. Cut dough with 3-inch round cookie or biscuit cutter. Reroll dough scraps and cut out additional rounds.

3. Preheat oven to 425°F. Place about 2 teaspoons chicken mixture on each round. Brush edges lightly with water. Fold one side of dough over filling to form half circle; pinch edges to seal.

4. Arrange empanadas on parchment-lined baking sheets; brush lightly with egg. Bake 16 to 18 minutes or until lightly browned. Serve with additional salsa, if desired.   *Makes 10 appetizer servings*

Note: Empanadas can be prepared ahead of time and frozen. Simply wrap unbaked empanadas in foil and freeze. To bake, unwrap and follow directions in step 4, baking 18 to 20 minutes.

Barbecue Chicken Sliders

1 pound (16 ounces) ground chicken
½ cup barbecue sauce, divided
   Nonstick cooking spray
4 slices sharp Cheddar cheese, quartered
4 to 6 slices whole wheat sandwich bread
   Lettuce leaves

1. Combine chicken and ¼ cup barbecue sauce in medium bowl. Shape mixture into 16 meatballs.

2. Spray nonstick grill pan or large skillet with cooking spray; heat over medium-high heat. Place meatballs in pan; press with spatula to make patties. Cook 6 minutes per side or until chicken is no longer pink in center. Top with cheese.

3. Meanwhile, cut bread slices into circles or quarters; toast to desired doneness.

4. Top bread with lettuce and burgers; serve with remaining barbecue sauce. *Makes 16 burgers*

Angel Wings

1 can (10¾ ounces) condensed tomato soup, undiluted
¾ cup water
¼ cup packed brown sugar
2½ tablespoons balsamic vinegar
2 tablespoons chopped shallots
12 chicken wings

Slow Cooker Directions

1. Combine soup, water, brown sugar, vinegar and shallots in slow cooker; mix well.

2. Add chicken wings; stir to coat with sauce. Cover; cook on LOW 5 to 6 hours or until cooked through. *Makes 4 servings*

Dijon Chicken Skewers

  1 cup barbecue sauce
  ¼ cup yellow mustard
  1 pound chicken tenders (about 12)
    Salt and black pepper

1. Soak 10 to 12 (10- to 12-inch) wooden skewers 20 minutes in cold water to prevent scorching. Preheat broiler.

2. Combine barbecue sauce and mustard in medium bowl. Weave chicken tenders onto skewers; season with salt and pepper. Brush each skewer with sauce mixture. Discard any remaining sauce.

3. Broil skewers 3 minutes. Turn and broil 3 to 5 minutes or until chicken is no longer pink in center. *Makes 10 to 12 skewers*

Prep Time: 20 minutes
Cook Time: about 8 minutes

note

Chicken tenders, also known as supremes, are the lean, tender strips of rib meat that are found on the underside of the breast. They are skinless, boneless and have very little waste.

Dijon Chicken Skewers

Chicken Parmesan Stromboli

1 pound boneless, skinless chicken breast halves
½ teaspoon salt
¼ teaspoon ground black pepper
2 teaspoons olive oil
2 cups shredded mozzarella cheese (about 8 ounces)
1 jar (1 pound 10 ounces) RAGÚ® Chunky Pasta Sauce, divided
2 tablespoons grated Parmesan cheese
1 tablespoon finely chopped fresh parsley
1 pound fresh or thawed frozen bread dough

1. Preheat oven to 400°F. Season chicken with salt and pepper. In 12-inch skillet, heat olive oil over medium-high heat and brown chicken. Remove chicken from skillet and let cool; pull into large shreds.

2. In medium bowl, combine chicken, mozzarella cheese, ½ cup Ragú Chunky Pasta Sauce, Parmesan cheese and parsley; set aside.

3. On greased jelly-roll pan, press dough to form 12×10-inch rectangle. Arrange chicken mixture down center of dough. Cover filling bringing one long side into center, then overlap with the other long side; pinch seam to seal. Fold in ends and pinch to seal. Arrange on pan, seam-side down. Gently press in sides to form 12×4-inch loaf. Bake 35 minutes or until dough is cooked and golden. Cut stromboli into slices. Heat remaining pasta sauce and serve with stromboli. *Makes 6 servings*

Chicken Parmesan Stromboli

Buffalo Chicken Tenders

3 tablespoons hot sauce

½ teaspoon paprika

¼ teaspoon ground red pepper

1 pound chicken tenders

½ cup blue cheese dressing

¼ cup sour cream

2 tablespoons crumbled blue cheese

1 medium green or red bell pepper, cut lengthwise into ½-inch-thick slices

1. Preheat oven to 375°F. Combine hot sauce, paprika and ground red pepper in small bowl; brush on all surfaces of chicken. Place chicken in greased 11×7-inch baking dish. Cover; marinate in refrigerator 30 minutes.

2. Bake, uncovered, about 15 minutes or until chicken is no longer pink in center.

3. Combine blue cheese dressing, sour cream and blue cheese in small serving bowl. Serve dip with chicken and pepper slices.

Makes 10 servings

note

Buffalo chicken wings originated in a New York bar. The extra-spicy wings were deep fried and served with blue cheese dressing. This lower-fat version replaces the wings with chicken tenders and is baked instead of fried.

Buffalo Chicken Tenders

Crispy Tortilla Chicken

1½ cups crushed tortilla chips
1 package (about 1 ounce) taco seasoning mix
24 chicken drummettes (about 2 pounds)
Salsa (optional)

1. Preheat oven to 350°F. Spray baking sheet with nonstick cooking spray.

2. Combine tortilla chips and taco seasoning in large shallow bowl. Coat chicken with crumb mixture, turning to coat all sides. Shake off excess crumbs; place chicken on prepared baking sheet.

3. Bake about 40 minutes or until chicken is cooked through (165°F). Serve with salsa, if desired.   *Makes 2 dozen drummettes*

Variation: The recipe can also be prepared using 1 pound boneless skinless chicken breasts cut into 1-inch strips. Bake at 350°F about 20 minutes or until chicken is no longer pink in center.

note

To test bone-in chicken pieces, you should be able to insert a fork into the chicken with ease and the juices should run clear. The meat and juices nearest the bones might still be a little pink even though the chicken is cooked thoroughly. Boneless chicken pieces are done when the centers are no longer pink; you can determine this by simply cutting into the chicken with a paring knife.

Crispy Tortilla Chicken

Savory Chicken Satay

1 envelope LIPTON® RECIPE SECRETS® Onion Soup Mix
¼ cup BERTOLLI® Olive Oil
2 tablespoons firmly packed brown sugar
2 tablespoons SKIPPY® Peanut Butter
1 pound boneless, skinless chicken breasts, pounded and cut into thin strips
12 to 16 large wooden skewers, soaked in water

1. In large plastic bag, combine soup mix, olive oil, brown sugar and peanut butter. Add chicken and toss to coat well. Seal bag and marinate in refrigerator 30 minutes.

2. Remove chicken from marinade, discarding marinade. On skewers, thread chicken, weaving back and forth.

3. Grill or broil skewers until chicken is cooked through. Serve with favorite dipping sauces. *Makes 12 to 16 appetizers*

Prep Time: 15 minutes
Marinate Time: 30 minutes
Cook Time: 8 minutes

note

Pounding chicken breasts to a uniform thickness, usually ¼ inch, allows them to cook faster and more evenly. To flatten uncooked boneless chicken breasts, place one chicken breast half between two sheets of waxed paper or plastic wrap. Using the flat side of a meat mallet or a rolling pin, gently pound the chicken from the center to the outside until it is of the desired thickness.

Savory Chicken Satay

classic
clucks

Garlicky Oven-Fried Chicken Thighs

1 egg
2 tablespoons water
1 cup plain dry bread crumbs
1 teaspoon salt
1 teaspoon garlic powder
½ teaspoon black pepper
¼ teaspoon ground red pepper
8 chicken thighs (about 3 pounds)
Olive oil cooking spray

1. Preheat oven to 350°F.

2. Beat egg with water in shallow bowl. Mix bread crumbs with salt, garlic powder, black pepper and red pepper in separate shallow bowl.

3. Dip chicken thighs into egg mixture; turn to coat. Transfer to bread crumb mixture; press lightly to coat both sides. Place chicken, skin side up, on large baking sheet.

4. Lightly spray chicken with cooking spray. Bake 50 to 60 minutes or until browned and cooked through (165°F). *Do not turn chicken during cooking.*   *Makes 4 servings*

Variations: Substitute flavored bread crumbs for the plain bread crumbs and spices. Or, substitute your favorite dried herbs or spices for the garlic powder and red pepper. Thyme, sage, oregano or rosemary would be delicious, as would Cajun or Creole seasoning.

Lemon-Rosemary Roasted Chicken

- 1 (6- to 7-pound) chicken
- 1 teaspoon olive oil, divided
- 1 teaspoon salt, divided
- ¼ teaspoon black pepper
- 2 lemons
- 2½ teaspoons dried rosemary *or* 2 (4-inch) sprigs fresh rosemary, leaves chopped, divided
- 2 teaspoons butter, softened
- 1 large onion, cut into ½-inch slices
- ¾ cup chicken broth
- ½ teaspoon ground sage

1. Preheat oven to 450°F. Rub chicken with ½ teaspoon oil. Season with ½ teaspoon salt and pepper.

2. Pierce 1 lemon in several places with knife tip or fork; place in chicken cavity. Blend 2 teaspoons rosemary and butter in small bowl. Carefully loosen skin on breast. Gently smooth butter mixture under skin. Tie legs with kitchen twine, if desired.

3. Place onion slices in middle of roasting pan and place chicken on top. Roast 45 minutes. Tent breast with foil; roast 30 minutes more or until cooked through (165°F). Baste with pan drippings occasionally.

4. Transfer chicken to cutting board; let rest 10 minutes. Pour pan drippings into measuring cup; skim fat. Squeeze juice from second lemon into drippings.

5. Return drippings to roasting pan; add any drippings from chicken. Add remaining ½ teaspoon salt, ½ teaspoon rosemary, broth and sage. Simmer over medium-high heat 2 minutes, stirring to scrape up browned bits from bottom of pan. Carve chicken; serve with sauce.

Makes 8 to 10 servings

Cook's Tip: Using thick onion slices as a "rack" on which to set the chicken imparts flavor to the drippings. Clean-up is much easier, as well.

Lemon-Rosemary Roasted Chicken

Chicken Parmesan

½ cup all-purpose flour
¼ teaspoon salt
¼ teaspoon ground black pepper
¼ cup milk
2 eggs
¾ cup CREAM OF WHEAT® Hot Cereal (Instant, 1-minute, 2½-minute or 10-minute cook time), uncooked
¾ cup grated Parmesan cheese
4 boneless skinless chicken breasts (about 1 pound)
¼ cup olive oil
2 cups pasta sauce, divided
1½ cups shredded mozzarella cheese, divided
Grated Parmesan cheese (optional)

1. Preheat oven to 350°F. Blend flour, salt and pepper in shallow bowl; set aside. Combine milk and eggs in second shallow bowl; set aside. Blend Cream of Wheat and ¾ cup Parmesan cheese in third shallow bowl; set aside.

2. Heat oil in large skillet over medium heat. Flatten chicken breasts slightly to uniform thickness. Dip each chicken breast into flour mixture, covering both sides evenly; shake off excess flour. Dip into egg mixture, covering both sides evenly. Dip into Cream of Wheat mixture, covering both sides evenly; shake off excess coating.

3. Place chicken into skillet. Cook 4 minutes or until edges begin to brown. Turn chicken over and cook 5 minutes longer until lightly browned. Remove chicken from skillet.

4. Spread 1 cup pasta sauce in bottom of casserole dish; place chicken on top. Sprinkle ¾ cup mozzarella cheese over chicken and top with remaining 1 cup pasta sauce. Sprinkle on remaining ¾ cup mozzarella cheese. Bake 30 minutes. Remove from oven and garnish with Parmesan cheese, if desired. *Makes 4 servings*

Tip: For more variety in your menus, substitute peeled eggplant or sliced pork tenderloin for the chicken.

Prep Time: 20 minutes
Start to Finish Time: 50 minutes

Chicken Parmesan

Chicken Divan Casserole

- 1 cup uncooked rice
- 1 cup coarsely shredded carrots
  Nonstick cooking spray
- 4 boneless skinless chicken breasts
- 2 tablespoons butter
- 3 tablespoons all-purpose flour
- ¼ teaspoon salt
  Black pepper
- 1 cup chicken broth
- ½ cup milk or half-and-half
- ¼ cup dry white wine
- ⅓ cup plus 2 tablespoons grated Parmesan cheese, divided
- 1 pound frozen broccoli florets

1. Preheat oven to 350°F. Lightly grease 12×8-inch baking dish.

2. Prepare rice according to package directions. Stir in carrots. Spoon mixture into prepared baking dish.

3. Spray large skillet with cooking spray. Heat over medium-high heat. Brown chicken breasts about 2 minutes on each side. Arrange over rice.

4. To prepare sauce, melt butter in 2-quart saucepan over medium heat. Whisk in flour, salt and pepper; cook and stir 1 minute. Gradually whisk in broth and milk. Cook and stir until mixture comes to a boil. Reduce heat; simmer 2 minutes. Stir in wine. Remove from heat. Stir in ⅓ cup cheese.

5. Arrange broccoli around chicken. Pour sauce over top. Sprinkle remaining 2 tablespoons cheese over chicken.

6. Cover with foil; bake 30 minutes. Remove foil; bake 10 to 15 minutes or until chicken is no longer pink in center and broccoli is crisp-tender. *Makes 6 servings*

Chicken and Wild Rice Soup

    3 cans (about 14 ounces each) chicken broth
    1 pound boneless skinless chicken breasts or thighs, cut
        into bite-size pieces
    2 cups water
    1 cup sliced celery
    1 cup diced carrots
    1 package (6 ounces) converted long grain and wild rice mix
        with seasoning packet
    ½ cup chopped onion
    ½ teaspoon black pepper
    2 teaspoons white vinegar (optional)
    1 tablespoon dried parsley flakes

Slow Cooker Directions

1. Combine broth, chicken, water, celery, carrots, rice with seasoning packet, onion and pepper in slow cooker; mix well.

2. Cover; cook on LOW 6 to 7 hours or on HIGH 4 to 5 hours or until chicken is tender.

3. Stir in vinegar, if desired. Sprinkle with parsley.

Makes 8 servings

Prep Time: 20 minutes
Cook Time: 6 to 7 hours

note

Wild rice isn't actually rice. It's the seed of a marsh grass native to the northern Great Lakes, where it was originally gathered by the Chippewa and other indigenous people. Wild rice has a chewy texture, a nutty, earthy flavor and is higher in protein than regular rice.

Chicken Cordon Bleu

- ¼ cup all-purpose flour
- 1 teaspoon paprika
- ½ teaspoon salt
- ¼ teaspoon black pepper
- 4 boneless chicken breasts, lightly pounded*
- 4 slices ham
- 4 slices Swiss cheese
- 2 tablespoons olive oil
- ½ cup white wine
- ½ cup chicken broth
- ½ cup half-and-half
- 2 tablespoons cornstarch

To flatten chicken, place it between two sheets of plastic wrap. Gently pound the chicken using the flat side of a meat mallet or heavy frying pan until it is about ¼ inch thick.

Slow Cooker Directions

1. Combine flour, paprika, salt and pepper in resealable food storage bag; shake well.

2. Place flattened chicken on cutting board, skin side down. Place 1 slice ham and 1 slice cheese on each piece. Fold chicken up to enclose filling and secure with toothpick. Place in bag with seasoned flour and shake gently to coat.

3. Heat oil in large skillet over medium-high heat. Brown chicken on all sides. Transfer to slow cooker.

4. Add wine to skillet; cook and stir to scrape up browned bits from bottom of skillet. Pour into slow cooker; add broth. Cover; cook on LOW 2 hours.

5. Remove chicken; keep warm. Mix together half-and-half and cornstarch in small bowl. Add to cooking liquid. Cover; cook on LOW 15 minutes or until sauce has thickened. Remove toothpicks before serving. *Makes 4 servings*

Chicken Cordon Bleu

Chicken Pot Pie

1½ **pounds chicken pieces, skinned**
1 **cup chicken broth**
½ **teaspoon salt**
¼ **teaspoon black pepper**
1 **to** 1½ **cups milk**
3 **tablespoons butter**
1 **medium onion, chopped**
1 **cup sliced celery**
⅓ **cup all-purpose flour**
2 **cups frozen mixed vegetables (such as broccoli, carrots and cauliflower), thawed**
1 **tablespoon chopped fresh parsley** *or* 1 **teaspoon dried parsley**
½ **teaspoon dried thyme**
1 **(9-inch) pie crust, at room temperature**
1 **egg, lightly beaten**

1. Combine chicken, broth, salt and pepper in large saucepan over medium-high heat. Bring to a boil. Reduce heat to low. Cover; simmer 30 minutes or until chicken is cooked through (165°F).

2. Remove chicken and let cool. Pour remaining chicken broth mixture into large measuring cup. Let stand; spoon off fat. Add enough milk to broth mixture to equal 2½ cups. Remove chicken from bones and cut into ½-inch pieces.

3. Melt butter in same saucepan over medium heat. Add onion and celery; cook and stir 3 minutes. Stir in flour until well blended. Gradually stir in broth mixture. Cook, stirring constantly, until sauce thickens and boils. Add chicken, vegetables, parsley and thyme. Pour into deep 1½-quart casserole.

4. Preheat oven to 400°F. Roll out crust 1 inch larger than diameter of casserole on lightly floured surface. Cut slits in crust to vent; place on top of casserole. Roll edges and cut away extra dough; flute edges. If desired, reroll scraps to cut into decorative designs; place on crust. Brush with egg. Bake about 30 minutes or until crust is golden brown and filling is bubbly.   *Makes 4 servings*

Variation: 2 cups diced cooked chicken, 1 can (about 14 ounces) chicken broth and ¼ teaspoon salt can be substituted for the first 3 ingredients.

Chicken Pot Pie

Chicken and Black Bean Chili

- 1 pound boneless skinless chicken thighs, cut into 1-inch chunks
- 2 teaspoons chili powder
- 2 teaspoons ground cumin
- ¾ teaspoon salt
- 1 green bell pepper, diced
- 1 small onion, chopped
- 3 cloves garlic, minced
- 1 can (about 14 ounces) diced tomatoes, undrained
- 1 cup chunky salsa
- 1 can (about 15 ounces) black beans, rinsed and drained

  Optional toppings: sour cream, diced ripe avocado, shredded Cheddar cheese, sliced green onions, chopped cilantro and crushed tortilla chips

Slow Cooker Directions

1. Combine chicken, chili powder, cumin and salt in slow cooker; toss to coat.

2. Add bell pepper, onion and garlic; mix well. Stir in tomatoes and salsa. Cover; cook on LOW 5 to 6 hours or on HIGH 2½ to 3 hours or until chicken is tender.

3. *Increase heat to HIGH.* Stir in beans. Cover; cook 5 to 10 minutes or until beans are heated through. Ladle into bowls; serve with desired toppings. *Makes 4 servings*

Chili powder is a spice blend typically made up of ground dried chilies, cloves, coriander, cumin, garlic and oregano.

Chicken and Black Bean Chili

Chicken Cassoulet

4 slices bacon

¼ cup all-purpose flour

Salt and black pepper

1¾ pounds bone-in chicken pieces

2 cooked chicken sausages (2¼ ounces each), cut into ¼-inch pieces

1½ cups diced red and green bell peppers (about 2 small bell peppers)

1 medium onion, chopped

2 cloves garlic, finely chopped

1 teaspoon dried thyme

1 teaspoon olive oil

2 cans (about 15 ounces each) cannellini or Great Northern beans, rinsed and drained

½ cup dry white wine

1. Preheat oven to 350°F. Cook bacon in large skillet over medium-high heat until crisp; drain on paper towels. Cut into 1-inch pieces.

2. Pour off all but 2 tablespoons fat from skillet. Place flour, salt and pepper in shallow bowl. Dip chicken pieces into flour mixture; shake off excess. Brown chicken in batches in skillet over medium-high heat; remove and set aside. Lightly brown sausages in same skillet; remove and set aside.

3. Add bell peppers, onion, garlic and thyme to skillet. Cook and stir over medium heat 5 minutes or until softened, adding oil as needed to prevent sticking. Transfer to 13×9-inch baking dish. Add beans; mix well. Top with chicken, sausages and bacon. Add wine to skillet; cook and stir over medium heat, scraping up browned bits from bottom of skillet. Pour over casserole.

4. Cover; bake 40 minutes. Uncover; bake 15 minutes or until chicken is cooked through (165°F). *Makes 6 servings*

Spicy Barbecued Chicken

  1 tablespoon paprika or smoked paprika
  1 teaspoon dried thyme
½ teaspoon salt
½ teaspoon dried sage
¼ teaspoon ground red pepper
¼ teaspoon black pepper
  1 whole chicken (3½ to 4 pounds), quartered
¾ cup ketchup
½ cup packed brown sugar
  2 tablespoons soy sauce
  2 tablespoons Worcestershire sauce
  1 clove garlic, minced

1. Combine paprika, thyme, salt, sage, red pepper and black pepper in small bowl. Press mixture onto all sides of chicken. Transfer chicken to large resealable food storage bag. Seal bag; refrigerate up to 24 hours.

2. For basting sauce, mix ketchup, brown sugar, soy sauce, Worcestershire sauce and garlic in small bowl.

3. Prepare grill for direct cooking. Place chicken on grid over medium heat. Grill, covered, 30 to 40 minutes or until cooked through (165°F), turning occasionally. Brush chicken generously with basting sauce during last 10 minutes of cooking. Serve with remaining sauce.   *Makes 4 servings*

note

It's best to leave the skin on chicken while grilling to preserve its natural moisture. The skin can be easily removed before serving or at the table, but much of the flavor is in the skin.

Basque Chicken with Peppers

1 whole chicken (4 pounds), cut into 8 pieces
Salt and black pepper
1½ tablespoons olive oil
1 onion, chopped
2 cloves garlic, minced
3 bell peppers (red, yellow and/or green), cut into strips
8 ounces brown mushrooms, halved
1 can (about 14 ounces) stewed tomatoes
½ cup chicken broth
½ cup red wine
3 ounces tomato paste
1 sprig fresh marjoram (optional)
1 teaspoon salt
1 teaspoon smoked paprika
½ teaspoon black pepper
4 ounces diced prosciutto
Hot cooked rice

Slow Cooker Directions

1. Season chicken with salt and pepper.

2. Heat oil in large skillet over medium-high heat. Add chicken in batches and brown well on all sides. Transfer to slow cooker.

3. Add onion and garlic to skillet. Cook and stir over medium-low heat 3 minutes or until softened. Add peppers and mushrooms to skillet; cook and stir 3 minutes more. Add tomatoes, broth, wine, tomato paste, marjoram, if desired, salt, paprika and black pepper to skillet. Simmer 3 to 4 minutes; pour over chicken in slow cooker.

4. Cover; cook on LOW 5 to 6 hours or on HIGH 4 hours or until chicken is cooked through. Sprinkle with prosciutto and serve with rice. *Makes 4 to 6 servings*

Basque Chicken with Peppers

Southern Buttermilk Fried Chicken

2 cups all-purpose flour
1½ teaspoons celery salt
1 teaspoon dried thyme
¾ teaspoon black pepper
½ teaspoon dried marjoram
1¾ cups buttermilk
2 cups vegetable oil
3 pounds chicken pieces

1. Combine flour, celery salt, thyme, pepper and marjoram in shallow bowl. Pour buttermilk into medium bowl.

2. Heat oil in heavy deep skillet over medium heat to 350°F.

3. Dip chicken into buttermilk, 1 piece at a time; shake off excess. Coat with flour mixture; shake off excess. Dip again in buttermilk and coat once more with flour mixture. Fry chicken in batches, skin side down, 10 to 12 minutes or until browned. Turn and fry 12 to 14 minutes or until cooked through (165°F). *Allow temperature of oil to return to 350°F between batches.* Drain chicken on paper towels.

Makes 4 servings

Buttermilk originally was the liquid leftover after butter was churned. Now it is made from milk to which a bacterial culture is added to produce the tangy flavor. Fresh milk can be soured and used as a substitute for buttermilk. To equal 1 cup of buttermilk, place 1 tablespoon lemon juice or distilled white vinegar in a measuring cup and add enough milk to measure 1 cup. Stir and let the mixture stand at room temperature for 5 minutes.

Southern Buttermilk Fried Chicken

Chicken Vesuvio

3 tablespoons all-purpose flour
1½ teaspoons dried oregano
1 teaspoon salt
½ teaspoon black pepper
1 chicken (3 or 4 pounds), cut up
2 tablespoons olive oil
4 small baking potatoes, cut into wedges
2 small onions, cut into thin wedges
4 cloves garlic, minced
¼ cup chicken broth
¼ cup dry white wine
¼ cup chopped parsley
Lemon wedges (optional)

Slow Cooker Directions

1. Combine flour, oregano, salt and pepper in large resealable food storage bag. Add chicken to bag several pieces at a time; shake to coat. Heat oil in large skillet over medium heat. Add chicken; cook 10 to 12 minutes or until browned on all sides.

2. Place potatoes, onion and garlic in slow cooker. Add broth and wine. Top with chicken pieces; pour pan juices from skillet over chicken. Cover; cook on LOW 6 to 7 hours or on HIGH 3 to 3½ hours or until chicken is cooked through and potatoes are tender.

3. Serve chicken and vegetables with juices. Sprinkle with parsley. Serve with lemon wedges.   *Makes 4 to 6 servings*

Chicken Vesuvio

grill greats

Southwestern Pineapple and Chicken

1 can (20 ounce) DOLE® Pineapple Slices
1 tablespoon lime juice
1 tablespoon vegetable oil
1½ teaspoons chili powder
½ teaspoon dried oregano leaves, crushed
1 garlic clove, finely chopped
5 boneless, skinless chicken breast halves

- Drain pineapple; reserve ½ cup juice.

- Combine reserved pineapple juice, lime juice, oil, chili, oregano and garlic in sealable plastic bag. Add chicken. Refrigerate and marinate 15 minutes.

- Grill or broil chicken and pineapple, brushing occasionally with reserved marinade, 5 to 8 minutes on each side or until chicken is no longer pink in center and pineapple is lightly browned. Discard any remaining marinade. *Makes 5 servings*

Southwestern Pineapple and Fish: Substitute 2 pounds fish steaks such as halibut, swordfish or sea bass for chicken. Prepare recipe as directed except grill 8 to 10 minutes on each side or until fish flakes with a fork.

Prep Time: 5 minutes
Marinate Time: 15 minutes
Grill Time: 10 minutes

Cumin BBQ Chicken

1 cup barbecue sauce
½ cup orange juice
3 tablespoons vegetable oil
2 tablespoons minced garlic
2 teaspoons ground coriander
2 teaspoons ground cumin
1 teaspoon black pepper
½ teaspoon salt
2 whole chickens (about 3½ pounds each), cut up

1. Combine barbecue sauce, orange juice, oil, garlic, coriander, cumin, pepper and salt in medium bowl; mix well. Reserve ¾ cup sauce.

2. Prepare grill for direct cooking. Place chicken on grid over medium heat. Grill, covered, 20 minutes, turning once. Brush lightly with sauce. Grill about 20 minutes more or until chicken is cooked through (165°F).

3. Serve with reserved ¾ cup sauce.   *Makes 8 servings*

Oven Method: Preheat oven to 375°F. Place chicken in large foil-lined shallow roasting pan. Prepare sauce; reserve ¾ cup. Brush chicken with remaining sauce. Bake 45 to 50 minutes or until chicken is cooked through. Baste chicken with sauce every 15 minutes. *Do not baste during last 5 minutes of baking.* Discard any remaining basting sauce. Serve with reserved ¾ cup sauce.

Cumin BBQ Chicken

Grilled Chipotle Chicken Sandwiches

1 medium lime, halved
4 boneless skinless chicken breasts, flattened slightly
½ cup sour cream
2 tablespoons mayonnaise
1 canned chipotle pepper in adobo sauce, minced
2 teaspoons adobo sauce
⅛ teaspoon salt
   Black pepper
2 slices Swiss cheese, cut in half diagonally
4 whole wheat hamburger buns
4 thin slices red onion
4 leaves romaine lettuce

1. Squeeze juice from half of lime evenly over chicken. Prepare grill for direct cooking.

2. Combine sour cream, mayonnaise, chipotle pepper, adobo sauce and salt in blender. Blend until smooth.

3. Place chicken on grid; grill over high heat 2 minutes. Turn and sprinkle with black pepper. Grill 2 minutes longer or until chicken is no longer pink in center. Move chicken to side of grill. Squeeze remaining lime half over chicken; top with cheese.

4. Place buns on grill; toast lightly. Spread with chipotle mixture. Top with onion, lettuce and chicken. *Makes 4 servings*

Grilled Chipotle Chicken Sandwich

Lime-Mustard Marinated Chicken

2 boneless skinless chicken breasts
¼ cup fresh lime juice
3 tablespoons honey mustard, divided
2 teaspoons olive oil
¼ teaspoon ground cumin
⅛ teaspoon garlic powder
⅛ teaspoon ground red pepper
¾ cup plus 2 tablespoons reduced-sodium chicken broth, divided
¼ cup uncooked rice
1 cup broccoli florets
⅓ cup matchstick carrots

1. Place chicken in large resealable food storage bag. Whisk together lime juice, 2 tablespoons mustard, oil, cumin, garlic powder and red pepper in small bowl. Pour mixture over chicken in bag. Seal bag; turn to coat. Marinate in refrigerator 2 hours.

2. Combine ¾ cup broth, rice and remaining 1 tablespoon mustard in small saucepan. Bring to a boil over high heat. Reduce heat. Cover; simmer 12 minutes or until rice is almost tender. Stir in broccoli, carrots and remaining 2 tablespoons broth. Cook, covered, 2 to 3 minutes or until vegetables are crisp-tender and rice is tender.

3. Meanwhile, prepare grill for direct cooking. Drain chicken; discard marinade. Grill chicken over medium heat, turning once, 10 to 13 minutes or until no longer pink in center. Serve chicken with rice mixture. *Makes 2 servings*

Hint: This marinade works well with other chicken cuts. Try boneless skinless thighs. They have a little more fat than breasts, so they tend to stay moist and tender.

Lime-Mustard Marinated Chicken

Grilled Chicken with Southern Barbecue Sauce

Nonstick cooking spray
½ **cup chopped onion (about 1 small)**
4 **cloves garlic, minced**
1 **can (16 ounces) tomato sauce**
¾ **cup water**
3 **tablespoons packed light brown sugar**
3 **tablespoons chili sauce**
2 **teaspoons chili powder**
2 **teaspoons dried thyme**
2 **teaspoons Worcestershire sauce**
¾ **teaspoon ground red pepper**
½ **teaspoon ground cinnamon**
½ **teaspoon black pepper**
6 **skinless bone-in chicken breasts (2¼ pounds)**

1. Spray medium nonstick skillet with cooking spray; heat over medium heat. Add onion and garlic; cook and stir about 5 minutes or until tender.

2. Stir in tomato sauce, water, sugar, chili sauce, chili powder, thyme, Worcestershire sauce, red pepper, cinnamon and black pepper; bring to a boil. Reduce heat to low and simmer, uncovered, 30 minutes or until mixture is reduced to about 1½ cups. Reserve ¾ cup sauce for basting.

3. Meanwhile, prepare grill for indirect cooking.

4. Grill chicken, covered, over medium heat 40 to 45 minutes or until chicken is cooked through (165°F), turning chicken several times and basting occasionally with reserved sauce.

5. Heat remaining sauce and serve with chicken.

Makes 6 servings

Grilled Chicken with Southern Barbecue Sauce

Thai Grilled Chicken

4 boneless skinless chicken breasts
¼ cup soy sauce
2 teaspoons minced garlic
½ teaspoon red pepper flakes
2 tablespoons honey
1 tablespoon fresh lime juice

1. Prepare grill for direct cooking. Place chicken in shallow baking dish. Combine soy sauce, garlic and pepper flakes in small bowl. Pour over chicken, turning to coat. Let stand 10 minutes.

2. Meanwhile, combine honey and lime juice in small bowl; blend well. Set aside.

3. Place chicken on grid over medium heat. Brush with marinade; discard remaining marinade. Grill, covered, 5 minutes. Brush both sides of chicken with honey mixture. Grill 5 minutes more or until chicken is no longer pink in center.   *Makes 4 servings*

Serving Suggestion: Serve with steamed rice, Asian vegetables and a fresh fruit salad.

Prep and Cook Time: 25 minutes

note

Fresh, uncooked chicken can be refrigerated for up to two days. If the chicken comes packaged in plastic bags or on plastic-sealed trays, it may be refrigerated in the original packaging. If the chicken comes wrapped in butcher paper, unwrap and repackage it airtight in plastic bags or plastic wrap. When you are ready to cook the chicken, rinse it under cold water, pat dry with paper towels and trim away any fat.

Thai Grilled Chicken

Garlic & Lemon Herb Marinated Chicken

3 to 4 pounds bone-in chicken pieces, skinned if desired
⅓ cup **French's®** Honey Dijon Mustard
⅓ cup lemon juice
⅓ cup olive oil
3 cloves garlic, minced
1 tablespoon grated lemon zest
1 tablespoon minced fresh thyme or rosemary
1 teaspoon coarse salt
½ teaspoon coarse black pepper

1. Place chicken into resealable plastic food storage bag. Combine remaining ingredients. Pour over chicken. Marinate in refrigerator 1 to 3 hours.

2. Remove chicken from marinade. Grill chicken over medium direct heat for 35 to 45 minutes until juices run clear near bone (165°F). Serve with additional mustard on the side.

Makes 4 servings

Tip: This marinade is also great on whole chicken or pork chops.

Prep Time: 10 minutes
Cook Time: 45 minutes
Marinate Time: 1 hour

note

Because chicken has a mild flavor, marinades help give it some zing. Marinating can be completed in as little as 20 to 30 minutes, but the longer the chicken marinates, the more flavorful it will be. However, chicken should not be left in acidic marinades for more than 3 hours since the acid breaks down tissue and the flesh can become mushy.

Garlic & Lemon Herb Marinated Chicken

Grilled Chicken with Spicy Black Beans & Rice

1 boneless skinless chicken breast
½ teaspoon Caribbean jerk seasoning
½ teaspoon olive oil
¼ cup finely diced green bell pepper
2 teaspoons chipotle chili powder
¾ cup hot cooked rice
½ cup rinsed and drained canned black beans
2 tablespoons diced pimiento
1 tablespoon chopped pimiento-stuffed green olives
1 tablespoon chopped onion
1 tablespoon chopped fresh cilantro (optional)
Lime wedges (optional)

1. Spray grid of grill with nonstick cooking spray; prepare grill for direct cooking. Rub chicken with jerk seasoning. Grill over medium heat 8 to 10 minutes or until no longer pink in center, turning once.

2. Meanwhile, heat oil in medium saucepan or skillet over medium heat. Add bell pepper and chili powder; cook and stir until peppers are soft.

3. Add rice, beans, pimiento and olives to saucepan. Cook about 3 minutes or until hot.

4. Serve bean mixture with chicken. Top bean mixture with onion and cilantro, if desired. Garnish with lime wedges.

Makes 2 servings

Blue Cheese Stuffed Chicken Breasts

½ cup (2 ounces) crumbled blue cheese
2 tablespoons butter, softened, divided
¾ teaspoon dried thyme
   Salt and black pepper
4 bone-in chicken breasts with skin
1 tablespoon lemon juice
½ teaspoon paprika

1. Prepare grill for direct cooking. Combine blue cheese, 1 tablespoon butter and thyme in small bowl until blended. Season with salt and pepper.

2. Loosen skin over chicken by pushing fingers between skin and meat, taking care not to tear skin. Spread blue cheese mixture under skin; massage skin to evenly spread cheese mixture.

3. Place chicken, skin side down, on grid over medium heat. Grill, covered, 15 minutes. Meanwhile, melt remaining 1 tablespoon butter in small bowl; stir in lemon juice and paprika. Turn chicken; brush with lemon juice mixture. Grill 15 to 20 minutes more or until chicken is cooked through (165°F). *Makes 4 servings*

Serving Suggestion: Serve with steamed new potatoes and broccoli.

Prep and Cook Time: 40 minutes

Sesame Hoisin Beer-Can Chicken

1 can (12 ounces) beer
½ cup hoisin sauce
2 tablespoons honey
1 tablespoon soy sauce
1 teaspoon chili garlic sauce
½ teaspoon dark sesame oil
1 chicken (3½ to 4 pounds)

1. Prepare grill for indirect cooking. Combine 2 tablespoons beer, hoisin sauce, honey, soy sauce, chili garlic sauce and sesame oil in small bowl. With your fingers, gently loosen skin of chicken over breast meat, legs and thighs. Spoon some hoisin mixture into cavity and under skin. Pour off beer until can is two-thirds full. Hold chicken upright with opening of cavity pointing down. Insert beer can into cavity.

2. Stand chicken upright on can over drip pan. Spread legs slightly to help support chicken. Cover; grill over medium heat 30 minutes. Brush chicken with remaining hoisin mixture. Cover; grill 45 to 60 minutes or until chicken is cooked through (165°F). Use metal tongs to lift chicken to cutting board and let rest, standing up, 5 minutes. Carefully remove beer can and discard. Carve chicken and serve. *Makes 2 servings*

note

Beer-can chicken might sound strange, but this technique produces a very tender and flavorful chicken. The beer adds moisture to the meat and keeps it juicy, while the yeast and malt in beer help create a nice crispy skin. You can buy a small metal stand to secure the chicken in place so it will not tip over on the grill. They are inexpensive and available at many hardware stores.

Sesame Hoisin Beer-Can Chicken

Chicken with Mango-Cherry Chutney

1½ cups chopped fresh mangoes, divided (about 2 large mangoes)
⅓ cup dried tart cherries
1 tablespoon packed brown sugar
1 tablespoon cider vinegar
½ teaspoon mustard seeds, slightly crushed
¼ teaspoon salt, divided
¼ cup sliced green onions
1½ teaspoons Chinese 5-spice powder
4 boneless skinless chicken breasts *or* 8 small boneless skinless chicken thighs (about 1 pound total)

1. Prepare grill for direct cooking.

2. Combine ½ cup mango, cherries, brown sugar, vinegar, mustard seeds and ⅛ teaspoon salt in medium saucepan; cook and stir over medium-low heat 5 minutes or until mango is tender. Slightly mash mango. Stir in remaining 1 cup mango and green onions. Keep warm.

3. Lightly sprinkle 5-spice powder and remaining ⅛ teaspoon salt on both sides of chicken. Grill chicken over medium heat 7 to 10 minutes or until chicken is no longer pink in center, turning once.

4. Serve mango mixture over chicken. *Makes 4 servings*

Chicken with Mango-Cherry Chutney

Grilled Chicken with Chili Beer Baste

2 tablespoons vegetable oil
1 small onion, chopped
1 clove garlic, minced
$\frac{1}{2}$ cup ketchup
2 chipotle peppers in adobo sauce, minced
2 tablespoons brown sugar
2 teaspoons chili powder
1 teaspoon dry mustard
$\frac{1}{2}$ teaspoon salt
$\frac{1}{2}$ teaspoon black pepper
3 bottles (12 ounces each) pilsner beer
$\frac{1}{2}$ cup tomato juice
$\frac{1}{4}$ cup Worcestershire sauce
1 tablespoon lemon juice
2 whole chickens (about 3$\frac{1}{2}$ pounds each), cut up

1. To make Chili Beer Baste, heat oil in large saucepan over medium heat. Add onion and garlic; cook and stir until onion is tender. Combine ketchup, chipotle peppers, brown sugar, chili powder, mustard, salt and black pepper in medium bowl. Add 1 bottle beer, tomato juice, Worcestershire sauce and lemon juice; whisk until well blended. Pour mixture into saucepan with onion and garlic. Bring to a simmer; cook until sauce is thickened slightly and reduced to about 2 cups. Let cool. Refrigerate overnight.

2. Place chicken pieces in 2 large resealable food storage bags. Pour remaining 2 bottles beer over chickens; seal bags. Refrigerate 8 hours or overnight.

3. Prepare grill for direct cooking. Remove chickens from beer; discard beer. Place chickens on grid over medium heat. Grill 15 to 20 minutes, turning occasionally.

4. Remove Chili Beer Baste from refrigerator; set aside 1 cup. Continue grilling chicken, basting frequently, 10 minutes or until cooked through (165°F). Warm reserved Chili Beer Baste and serve with chicken. *Makes 8 servings*

Grilled Chicken with Chili Beer Baste

ethnic birds

Provençal Lemon and Olive Chicken

2 cups chopped onions
8 skinless chicken thighs (about 2½ pounds)
1 lemon, thinly sliced and seeds removed
1 cup pitted green olives
1 tablespoon olive brine from jar or white vinegar
2 teaspoons herbes de Provence
1 bay leaf
½ teaspoon salt
⅛ teaspoon black pepper
1 cup chicken broth
½ cup minced fresh parsley

Slow Cooker Directions

1. Place onions in slow cooker. Arrange chicken thighs over onions. Place lemon slice on each thigh. Add olives, brine, herbes de Provence, bay leaf, salt and pepper. Slowly pour in broth.

2. Cover; cook on LOW 5 to 6 hours or on HIGH 3 to 3½ hours or until chicken is tender. Remove and discard bay leaf. Stir in parsley before serving. *Makes 8 servings*

Note: To skin chicken easily, grasp skin with paper towel and pull firmly.

Prep Time: 15 minutes
Cook Time: 5 to 6 hours (LOW) or 3 to 3½ hours (HIGH)

Dim Sum Baked Buns

6 to 8 dried shiitake mushrooms
3 green onions, minced
2 tablespoons plum sauce
1 tablespoon hoisin sauce
   Nonstick cooking spray
8 ounces ground chicken
4 cloves garlic, minced
1 tablespoon minced fresh ginger
8 frozen bread dough rolls (12 ounces), thawed
1 egg, beaten
¾ teaspoon sesame seeds

1. Place mushrooms in small bowl. Cover with warm water; let stand 30 minutes. Rinse well and drain, squeezing out excess water. Cut off and discard stems. Finely chop caps. Combine mushrooms, green onions, plum sauce and hoisin sauce in large bowl.

2. Spray medium nonstick skillet with cooking spray; heat over high heat. Add chicken; cook without stirring 1 to 2 minutes or until no longer pink. Add garlic and ginger; cook and stir 2 minutes more. Add mushroom mixture; mix well.

3. Spray 2 baking sheets with cooking spray. Lightly flour hands and work surface. Cut each roll in half; roll each piece into a ball. Shape each piece between hands to form disk. Press edge of disk between thumb and forefinger, working in circular motion to form circle 3 to 3½ inches in diameter. (Center of disk should be thicker than edges.)

4. Place disk flat on work surface. Place 1 generous tablespoon filling in center. Lift edge of dough up and around filling; pinch edge of dough together to seal. Place seam side down on baking sheet. Repeat with remaining dough and filling.

5. Cover buns with towel; let rise in warm place 45 minutes or until buns have doubled in size.

6. Meanwhile, preheat oven to 375°F. Brush buns with egg, then sprinkle with sesame seeds. Bake 16 to 18 minutes or until buns are golden brown. *Makes 16 buns*

Dim Sum Baked Buns

Greek Roast Chicken

1 whole roasting chicken (4 to 5 pounds)
3 tablespoons olive oil, divided
2 tablespoons chopped fresh rosemary leaves, plus fresh sprigs
2 cloves garlic, minced
1 lemon
1¼ teaspoons salt, divided
½ teaspoon black pepper, divided
1 can (about 14 ounces) chicken broth, divided
2 large sweet potatoes, cut into thick wedges
1 medium red onion, cut into ¼-inch wedges
1 pound fresh asparagus spears, trimmed

1. Preheat oven to 425°F. Place chicken, breast side up, in shallow roasting pan.

2. Combine 2 tablespoons oil, chopped rosemary and garlic in small bowl; brush over chicken.

3. Grate 1 teaspoon peel from lemon; set aside. Cut lemon into quarters; squeeze juice over chicken and place rinds and rosemary sprigs in chicken cavity. Sprinkle ¾ teaspoon salt and ¼ teaspoon pepper over chicken. Pour 1 cup broth into bottom of roasting pan; roast 30 minutes.

4. *Reduce oven temperature to 375°F.* Arrange sweet potatoes and onion wedges in single layer around chicken in roasting pan. Drizzle remaining broth and 1 tablespoon oil over vegetables; roast 15 minutes.

5. Arrange asparagus spears in roasting pan. Sprinkle remaining ½ teaspoon salt and ¼ teaspoon pepper over vegetables. Roast 10 minutes or until chicken is cooked through (165°F) and vegetables are tender. Transfer chicken to cutting board. Tent with foil; let stand 10 to 15 minutes.

6. Sprinkle reserved lemon peel over chicken. Serve with vegetables and pan juices.   *Makes 8 servings*

Chicken Teriyaki

8 large chicken drumsticks (about 2 pounds)
⅓ cup teriyaki sauce
2 tablespoons brandy or apple juice
1 green onion, minced
1 tablespoon vegetable oil
1 teaspoon ground ginger
½ teaspoon sugar
¼ teaspoon garlic powder
    Sweet and sour sauce (optional)

1. Remove skin from drumsticks, if desired, by pulling skin toward end of leg using paper towel; discard skin.

2. Place chicken in large resealable food storage bag. Combine teriyaki sauce, brandy, green onion, oil, ginger, sugar and garlic powder in small bowl; pour over chicken. Close bag securely; turn to coat. Marinate in refrigerator at least 1 hour or overnight, turning occasionally.

3. Prepare grill for indirect cooking.

4. Drain chicken; reserve marinade. Place chicken on grid directly over drip pan. Grill, covered, over medium-high heat 60 minutes or until chicken is cooked through (165°F), turning and brushing with reserved marinade every 20 minutes. *Do not brush with marinade during last 5 minutes of grilling.* Discard remaining marinade. Serve with sweet and sour sauce, if desired.   *Makes 4 servings*

Sauces and marinades add flavor and moisture to grilled foods. Brush foods with sauces during the last 30 minutes of cooking to avoid excess charring. For food safety, allow the meat or poultry to cook on the grill at least 5 minutes after the last application of sauce.

Chicken Normandy Style

2 tablespoons butter, divided
3 cups thinly sliced apples, such as Fuji or Braeburn (about 3 apples)
1 pound ground chicken
¼ cup apple brandy or apple juice
1 can (10¾ ounces) condensed cream of chicken soup, undiluted
¼ cup chopped green onions
2 teaspoons minced fresh sage leaves *or* ½ teaspoon dried sage
¼ teaspoon black pepper
1 package (12 ounces) egg noodles, cooked and drained

1. Preheat oven to 350°F. Grease 9-inch square casserole.

2. Melt 1 tablespoon butter in large nonstick skillet. Add apples; cook and stir over medium heat 7 to 10 minutes or until tender. Remove apples from skillet.

3. Brown chicken in same skillet over medium heat, stirring to break up meat. Stir in brandy; cook 2 minutes. Stir in soup, green onions, sage, pepper and apple slices. Reduce heat and simmer 5 minutes.

4. Melt remaining 1 tablespoon butter and toss with noodles. Spoon into prepared casserole. Top with chicken mixture. Bake 15 minutes or until hot. *Makes 4 servings*

Note: Ground turkey, ground pork or tofu crumbles can be substituted for chicken, if desired.

Chicken Normandy Style

Grilled Chicken Adobo

½ cup chopped onion
⅓ cup lime juice
6 cloves garlic, coarsely chopped
1 teaspoon ground cumin
1 teaspoon dried oregano
½ teaspoon dried thyme
¼ teaspoon ground red pepper
6 boneless skinless chicken breasts
3 tablespoons chopped fresh cilantro (optional)

1. Combine onion, lime juice and garlic in food processor. Process until onion is finely minced. Transfer to resealable food storage bag. Add cumin, oregano, thyme and red pepper; knead bag until blended. Place chicken in bag; press out air and seal. Turn to coat chicken with marinade. Refrigerate 30 minutes or up to 4 hours.

2. Spray grid with nonstick cooking spray. Prepare grill for direct cooking. Remove chicken from marinade; discard marinade. Place chicken on grid over medium heat. Grill 5 to 7 minutes on each side or until chicken is no longer pink in center. Transfer to clean serving platter and garnish with cilantro. *Makes 6 servings*

note

Adobo, a richly flavored paste of garlic, onion, ground dried chiles and herbs, is used as a marinade or sauce for chicken and pork throughout Latin America and in the Philippines. The presence of an acid, usually lime juice or vinegar, helps to tenderize the meat and adds another dimension of flavor.

Grilled Chicken Adobo

Italian Sausage-Stuffed Chicken Breasts

   Nonstick cooking spray
   4 ounces bulk Italian sausage
   ½ cup finely chopped green bell pepper
   ½ cup finely chopped yellow onion
   ½ teaspoon dried basil
   2 tablespoons plain dry bread crumbs
   2 boneless chicken breasts, pounded to ¼-inch thickness
   ⅔ cup pasta sauce
   2 slices provolone cheese
   Grated Parmesan cheese (optional)

1. Preheat oven to 350°F.

2. Coat medium nonstick skillet with cooking spray; heat over medium heat. Add sausage; brown 3 minutes, stirring to break up meat.

3. Add bell pepper, onion and basil; cook and stir 2 minutes. Let cool; stir in bread crumbs.

4. Line baking pan with foil. Place chicken breasts on pan; spoon sausage mixture in center of chicken. Roll up chicken around filling and place seam side down. Secure with toothpicks, if necessary. Spoon half of pasta sauce over rolls.

5. Bake 22 to 25 minutes or until chicken is cooked through (165°F). Top with provolone cheese; bake 5 minutes or until cheese melts. Remove toothpicks before serving. Sprinkle with Parmesan cheese, if desired. Serve with remaining pasta sauce.   *Makes 2 servings*

Grilled Chicken with Chimichurri Salsa

4 boneless skinless chicken breasts
½ cup plus 4 teaspoons olive oil, divided
Salt and black pepper
½ cup finely chopped parsley
¼ cup white wine vinegar
2 tablespoons finely chopped onion
3 cloves garlic, minced
1 jalapeño pepper,* finely chopped
2 teaspoons dried oregano

*Jalapeño peppers can sting and irritate the skin, so wear rubber gloves when handling peppers and do not touch your eyes.

1. Prepare grill for direct cooking.

2. Brush chicken with 4 teaspoons oil; season with salt and pepper. Place on grid over medium heat. Grill, covered, 10 to 16 minutes or until chicken is no longer pink in center, turning once.

3. For salsa, combine parsley, remaining ½ cup oil, vinegar, onion, garlic, jalapeño pepper and oregano. Season with salt and pepper. Serve over chicken.   *Makes 4 servings*

note

Chimichurri is a thick herb sauce that has a fresh, green color. Originating in Argentina, it is popular throughout Latin America with grilled meats and many other dishes. Try it with grilled steak or fish as well as chicken. It will keep refrigerated for 24 hours.

Chicken Curry

2 boneless skinless chicken breasts, cut into ¾-inch pieces
1 cup coarsely chopped apple, divided
1 small onion, sliced
3 tablespoons raisins
1 clove garlic, minced
1 teaspoon curry powder
¼ teaspoon ground ginger
⅓ cup water
1½ teaspoons chicken bouillon granules
1½ teaspoons all-purpose flour
¼ cup sour cream
½ teaspoon cornstarch
½ cup uncooked rice
   Chopped green onion (optional)

Slow Cooker Directions

1. Combine chicken, ¾ cup apple, onion, raisins, garlic, curry powder and ginger in slow cooker. Combine water and bouillon granules in small bowl until dissolved. Stir in flour until smooth. Add to slow cooker. Cover; cook on LOW 3½ to 4 hours or until onion is tender and chicken is cooked through.

2. Combine sour cream and cornstarch in large bowl. Transfer all cooking liquid from chicken mixture to sour cream mixture; stir until combined. Stir mixture back into slow cooker. Cover; let stand 5 to 10 minutes or until sauce is heated through.

3. Meanwhile, cook rice according to package directions. Serve chicken curry over rice; garnish with remaining ¼ cup apple and green onion. *Makes 2 servings*

Chicken Curry

Chicken Parmesan

2 cups tomato sauce
1 egg
¾ cup plain dry bread crumbs
½ cup grated Parmesan cheese
¼ teaspoon salt
¼ teaspoon black pepper
1½ pounds chicken tenders (about 12 tenders)
3 tablespoons olive oil
8 ounces fresh mozzarella cheese, cut into thin slices

1. Preheat broiler. Spread tomato sauce in 13×9-inch baking pan.

2. Beat egg in shallow dish. Combine bread crumbs, Parmesan, salt and pepper in another shallow dish.

3. Dip chicken tenders into egg, turning to coat; shake off excess. Dip into crumb mixture, turning to coat.

4. Heat oil in large nonstick skillet over medium-high heat. Cook chicken in batches about 5 minutes or until golden brown, turning once.

5. Arrange chicken in single layer on tomato sauce. Top with mozzarella slices. Broil 6 inches from heat 5 to 7 minutes or until cheese is melted and beginning to brown.   *Makes 4 servings*

Cook's Tip: To keep your hands from becoming breaded too, use one hand to dip the chicken pieces into the egg and the other hand to coat them with the crumbs.

Chicken Parmesan

Tandoori-Style Chicken with Cucumber Raita

1½ pounds chicken thighs, skin removed
1 small onion, coarsely chopped
⅓ cup plain yogurt
1 tablespoon tomato paste
2 cloves garlic, coarsely chopped
2 teaspoons chopped fresh ginger
½ jalapeño pepper
1 teaspoon garam masala*
1 teaspoon paprika
Grated peel of ½ lemon
Cucumber Raita (recipe follows)
6 rounds whole wheat pita bread

Garam masala is an Indian spice blend which includes warm spices such as cinnamon, black pepper, coriander, cardamom, nutmeg and others.

1. Lightly score each chicken thigh twice with sharp knife; place in large heavy-duty resealable food storage bag.

2. Place onion, yogurt, tomato paste, garlic, ginger, jalapeño pepper, garam masala, paprika and lemon peel in food processor; process until smooth. Add to chicken in bag; seal bag and turn to coat chicken thoroughly. Refrigerate 4 hours or overnight.

3. Prepare Cucumber Raita. Prepare grill for direct cooking.

4. Remove chicken from bag and discard marinade. Grill chicken, covered, over medium heat 20 to 25 minutes or until chicken is cooked through (165°F), turning once. Serve with Cucumber Raita and pitas. *Makes 6 servings*

Cucumber Raita

1 cup plain yogurt
½ cup finely chopped seeded cucumber
1 tablespoon minced fresh mint leaves
1 clove garlic, minced
¼ teaspoon salt

Combine all ingredients in small bowl. Cover and refrigerate until ready to use. *Makes 6 servings*

Coq au Vin & Pasta

4 large or 8 small chicken thighs (2 to 2½ pounds), trimmed of
    excess fat
2 teaspoons rotisserie or herb chicken seasoning*
1 tablespoon margarine or butter
3 cups (8 ounces) halved or quartered mushrooms
1 medium onion, coarsely chopped
½ cup dry white wine or vermouth
1 (4.9-ounce) package PASTA RONI® Homestyle Chicken Flavor
½ cup sliced green onions

1 teaspoon paprika and 1 teaspoon garlic salt can be substituted.

1. Sprinkle meaty side of chicken with rotisserie seasoning. In large skillet over medium-high heat, melt margarine. Add chicken, seasoned-side down; cook 3 minutes. Reduce heat to medium-low; turn chicken over.

2. Add mushrooms, onion and wine. Cover; simmer 15 to 18 minutes or until chicken is no longer pink inside. Remove chicken from skillet; set aside.

3. In same skillet, bring 1 cup water to a boil. Stir in pasta, green onions and Special Seasonings. Place chicken over pasta. Reduce heat to medium-low. Cover; gently boil 6 to 8 minutes or until pasta is tender. Let stand 3 to 5 minutes before serving.

Makes 4 servings

Prep Time: 10 minutes
Cook Time: 30 minutes

note

Coq au Vin, meaning "rooster in wine", is a popular rustic French dish. It consists of chicken, wine, mushrooms and often additions such as salt pork and garlic. Variations of the dish can be found throughout France that use regional wine.

Japanese Fried Chicken on Watercress

1 pound boneless skinless chicken breasts, cut into 2-inch pieces
3 tablespoons tamari or soy sauce
2 tablespoons sake
3 cloves garlic, minced
1 teaspoon minced fresh ginger
　Oil for deep frying
⅓ cup cornstarch
3 tablespoons all-purpose flour

Salad
¼ cup unseasoned rice vinegar
3 teaspoons tamari or soy sauce
1 teaspoon dark sesame oil
2 bunches watercress, trimmed of tough stems
1 pint grape tomatoes, halved

1. Place chicken in resealable food storage bag. Mix 3 tablespoons tamari, sake, garlic and ginger in small bowl. Pour over chicken and marinate in refrigerator at least 30 minutes, turning bag occasionally.

2. Meanwhile, heat at least 1½ inches oil to 350°F in deep heavy saucepan over medium-high heat. Combine cornstarch and flour in shallow dish. Drain chicken and discard marinade. Roll chicken pieces in cornstarch mixture and shake off excess.

3. Deep fry chicken in batches 4 to 6 minutes or until golden and no longer pink in center. (Do not crowd pan.) Drain on paper towels.

4. For salad dressing, whisk together vinegar, 3 teaspoons tamari and sesame oil in small bowl. Arrange watercress and tomatoes on serving plates; drizzle with dressing and top with chicken.

Makes 4 servings

Japanese Fried Chicken on Watercress

Chicken Marsala with Fettuccine

4 boneless skinless chicken breasts
  Salt and black pepper
1 tablespoon vegetable oil
1 onion, chopped
½ cup marsala wine
2 packages (6 ounces each) sliced brown mushrooms
½ cup chicken broth
2 teaspoons Worcestershire sauce
½ teaspoon salt
½ teaspoon black pepper
½ cup whipping cream
2 tablespoons cornstarch
8 ounces uncooked fettuccine
2 tablespoons chopped fresh parsley (optional)

Slow Cooker Directions

1. Coat 5- to 6-quart slow cooker with nonstick cooking spray. Season chicken with salt and pepper. Transfer to slow cooker.

2. Heat oil in large skillet over medium heat. Add onions; cook and stir until translucent. Add marsala and continue cooking 2 to 3 minutes or until mixture reduces slightly. Stir in mushrooms, broth, Worcestershire sauce, ½ teaspoon salt and ½ teaspoon pepper. Pour mixture over chicken. Cover; cook on HIGH 1½ to 1¾ hours or until chicken is no longer pink in center.

3. Transfer chicken to cutting board. Blend whipping cream and cornstarch in small bowl until smooth; stir into cooking liquid. Cover; cook 15 minutes or until mixture thickens. Season with salt and pepper.

4. Meanwhile, cook pasta according to package directions. Drain and transfer to large serving bowl. Slice chicken breasts and place on pasta. Top with sauce and garnish with parsley.

Makes 6 to 8 servings

Prep Time: 10 minutes
Cook Time: 1½ to 1¾ hours

Chicken Marsala with Fettuccine

Chicken Fried Rice

1 bag SUCCESS® Rice
½ pound boneless skinless chicken, cut into ½-inch pieces
½ teaspoon salt
¼ teaspoon pepper
2 tablespoons vegetable oil
1 clove garlic, minced
½ teaspoon grated fresh ginger
2 cups diagonally sliced green onions
1 cup sliced fresh mushrooms
2 tablespoons reduced-sodium soy sauce
1 teaspoon sherry
1 teaspoon Asian-style hot chili sesame oil (optional)

Prepare rice according to package directions.

Sprinkle chicken with salt and pepper; set aside. Heat vegetable oil in large skillet over medium-high heat. Add garlic and ginger; cook and stir 1 minute. Add chicken; stir-fry until no longer pink in center. Add green onions and mushrooms; stir-fry until tender. Stir in soy sauce, sherry and sesame oil. Add rice; heat thoroughly, stirring occasionally.   *Makes 6 servings*

note

You can often get a better price on boneless skinless chicken if you buy an extra large package. Pack the chicken you're not using immediately in heavy-duty freezer bags. Press as much air out of the package as possible, label it with the date and contents and freeze. Use the chicken within 4 months.

Chicken Fried Rice

lighter bites

Southwestern Chicken Salad

Salad

12 ounces chopped cooked chicken breast
1 can (about 15 ounces) black beans, rinsed and drained
1 can (8 ounces) diced water chestnuts
½ red bell pepper, diced
½ green bell pepper, diced
¼ red onion, chopped
½ cup chopped fresh cilantro
½ jalapeño pepper,* minced (optional)

Dressing

3 tablespoons cider vinegar
2 tablespoons olive oil
2 tablespoons orange juice
1 teaspoon ground cumin
½ teaspoon chili powder
½ teaspoon ground red pepper
¼ teaspoon salt

Jalapeño peppers can sting and irritate the skin, so wear rubber gloves when handling peppers and do not touch your eyes.

1. Stir together salad ingredients in large bowl.

2. Combine dressing ingredients in small container with tight-fitting lid. Shake until salt dissolves. Pour mixture over chicken salad. Toss to combine. *Makes 6 servings*

Grilled Chicken Salad with Creamy Tarragon Dressing

Creamy Tarragon Dressing (recipe follows)
1 pound chicken tenders
1 teaspoon Cajun or Creole seasoning
1 package (10 ounces) mixed salad greens
2 unpeeled apples, thinly sliced
1 cup alfalfa sprouts
2 tablespoons raisins

1. Prepare Creamy Tarragon Dressing.

2. Season chicken with Cajun seasoning. Spray grid with nonstick cooking spray. Prepare grill for direct cooking. Grill chicken over medium-high heat 5 to 7 minutes on each side or until no longer pink in center.

3. Divide salad greens among 4 large plates. Arrange chicken, apples and sprouts on top of greens. Sprinkle with raisins. Serve with dressing.   *Makes 4 servings*

Prep Time: 10 minutes
Cook Time: 14 minutes

Creamy Tarragon Dressing

½ **cup plain yogurt**
¼ **cup sour cream**
¼ **cup frozen apple juice concentrate**
1 **tablespoon minced fresh tarragon leaves**
1 **tablespoon spicy brown mustard**

Combine all ingredients in small bowl.   *Makes about 1 cup*

Grilled Chicken Salad with Creamy Tarragon Dressing

Rotini, Chicken and Spinach Salad

4 cups baby spinach
1½ cups diced cooked chicken breast, chilled
1⅓ cups cooked whole wheat rotini or macaroni
1 tablespoon minced fresh chives
1 teaspoon minced fresh dill
2 tablespoons reduced-sodium chicken broth
1 tablespoon olive oil
1½ teaspoons lemon juice
1 teaspoon Dijon mustard
⅛ teaspoon salt
⅛ teaspoon black pepper

1. Combine spinach, chicken, rotini, chives and dill in large salad bowl. Toss gently.

2. Whisk together broth, oil, lemon juice, mustard, salt and pepper in small bowl. Pour over salad mixture and toss gently.

Makes 4 servings

Citrus-Berry Chicken Salad

4 boneless skinless chicken breast halves
½ cup *French's®* Honey Mustard, divided
⅓ cup canola oil
2 tablespoons raspberry vinegar or balsamic vinegar
8 cups mixed salad greens, washed and torn
1 cup sliced strawberries or raspberries
1 orange, cut into sections

1. Coat chicken with ¼ *cup* mustard. Broil or grill 10 to 15 minutes or until chicken is no longer pink in center. Cut diagonally into slices.

2. In small bowl, whisk together remaining ¼ *cup* mustard, oil, vinegar and ¼ *teaspoon each salt and pepper.*

3. Arrange salad greens and fruit on serving plates. Top with chicken. Drizzle with dressing just before serving.

Makes 4 servings

Rotini, Chicken and Spinach Salad

White Bean and Chicken Ragoût

2 boneless skinless chicken thighs
2 small carrots, cut into ½-inch pieces
2 medium celery stalks, cut into ½-inch pieces
¼ medium onion, chopped
1 bay leaf
1 sprig fresh parsley
1 clove garlic
1 sprig fresh thyme
3 black peppercorns
1 can (about 15 ounces) cannellini beans, rinsed and drained
1 plum tomato, chopped
1 teaspoon herbes de Provence
½ teaspoon salt
⅛ teaspoon black pepper
1 teaspoon extra-virgin olive oil
1 tablespoon chopped fresh parsley
Grated peel of 1 lemon

1. Place chicken in medium saucepan; add water to cover. Add carrots, celery, onion, bay leaf, parsley, garlic, thyme and peppercorns. Bring to a boil over high heat; reduce heat to low. Simmer 15 to 20 minutes or until vegetables are tender.

2. Remove chicken from saucepan; let cool 5 minutes.

3. Drain vegetables; reserve broth. Discard bay leaf, parsley, garlic, thyme and peppercorns.

4. When cool enough to handle, cut chicken into bite-size pieces. Return chicken to saucepan with vegetables. Stir in beans and tomato. Add herbes de Provence, salt and black pepper.

5. Stir 1 cup broth into mixture; simmer 5 minutes.

6. Divide between 2 bowls; drizzle with oil. Sprinkle with chopped parsley and lemon peel. *Makes 2 servings*

Tuscan Chicken with White Beans

1 large fennel bulb (about ¾ pound)
1 teaspoon olive oil
1 teaspoon dried rosemary
½ teaspoon black pepper
½ pound boneless skinless chicken thighs, cut into ¾-inch pieces
1 can (about 14 ounces) stewed tomatoes, undrained
1 can (about 14 ounces) reduced-sodium chicken broth
1 can (about 15 ounces) cannellini beans, rinsed and drained
   Hot pepper sauce (optional)

1. Cut off and reserve ¼ cup chopped feathery fennel tops. Chop bulb into ½-inch pieces. Heat oil in large saucepan over medium heat. Add chopped fennel bulb; cook 5 minutes, stirring occasionally.

2. Sprinkle rosemary and pepper over chicken; add to saucepan. Cook and stir 2 minutes. Add tomatoes with juice and broth; bring to a boil. Reduce heat; simmer, covered, 10 minutes. Stir in beans; simmer, uncovered, 15 minutes or until chicken is cooked through and sauce thickens. Season to taste with hot pepper sauce. Ladle into 4 shallow bowls; top with reserved fennel tops.

Makes 4 servings

Prep Time: 15 minutes
Cook Time: 35 minutes

note

Fennel originated in southern Europe. It is most widely used as a vegetable in Mediterranean cuisines. The bulbous base, which slightly resembles celery in appearance and texture, is white to pale green with several slender stalks topped with a fringe of feathery green leaves. Fennel has a crisp texture and a slightly sweet licorice-like flavor, which mellows when cooked.

Chinese Chicken Salad

4 cups chopped bok choy

3 cups diced cooked chicken breast

1 cup shredded carrots

2 tablespoons minced fresh chives or green onions

2 tablespoons hot chili sauce with garlic*

1½ tablespoons peanut or canola oil

1 tablespoon balsamic vinegar

1 tablespoon soy sauce

1 teaspoon minced fresh ginger

Hot chili sauce with garlic is available in the Asian foods section of most supermarkets.

1. Place bok choy, chicken, carrots and chives in large bowl.

2. Combine chili garlic sauce, oil, vinegar, soy sauce and ginger in small bowl; mix well. Pour over chicken mixture; toss gently.

Makes 4 servings

Cobb Salad

1 package (10 ounces) mixed salad greens *or* 8 cups torn romaine lettuce

6 ounces cooked chicken breast, cut into bite-size pieces

1 tomato, seeded and chopped

2 hard-cooked eggs, cut into bite-size pieces

4 slices bacon, crisp-cooked and crumbled

1 ripe avocado, diced

1 large carrot, shredded

2 ounces blue cheese, crumbled

Prepared blue cheese or vinaigrette dressing

1. Place lettuce in serving bowl. Arrange chicken, tomato, eggs, bacon, avocado, carrot and cheese on top of lettuce.

2. Serve with dressing.

Makes 4 servings

Chinese Chicken Salad

Greek-Style Chicken and Bread Salad

2 slices stale crusty bread
1 clove garlic, halved
1 cup diced cooked chicken breast, chilled
1 cup halved cherry or grape tomatoes
1 small cucumber, peeled and diced
1/4 cup thinly sliced green onions
4 teaspoons lemon juice
2 1/2 tablespoons reduced-sodium chicken broth
1/2 teaspoon olive oil
1/4 teaspoon dried oregano
1/8 teaspoon salt
1/8 teaspoon black pepper

1. Toast or grill bread until lightly browned and crisp. Rub each bread slice with garlic. Tear into bite-size pieces. Combine bread, chicken, tomatoes, cucumber and green onions in large salad bowl. Toss gently.

2. Whisk together lemon juice, broth, oil, oregano, salt and pepper in small bowl. Pour over salad. Toss gently.   *Makes 2 servings*

Greek-Style Chicken and Bread Salad

Tortilla Soup

2 cans (about 14 ounces each) chicken broth
1 can (about 14 ounces) diced tomatoes with jalapeño peppers
2 cups chopped carrots
2 cups frozen corn, thawed
1½ cups chopped onions
1 can (8 ounces) tomato sauce
1 tablespoon chili powder
1 teaspoon ground cumin
¼ teaspoon garlic powder
2 cups chopped cooked chicken
Shredded Monterey Jack cheese
Tortilla chips, broken

Slow Cooker Directions

1. Combine broth, tomatoes, carrots, corn, onions, tomato sauce, chili powder, cumin and garlic powder in slow cooker. Cover; cook on LOW 6 to 8 hours.

2. Stir in chicken and cook until heated through. Ladle into bowls. Top each serving with cheese and tortilla chips.

Makes 6 servings

Prep Time: 10 minutes
Cook Time: 6 to 8 hours

note

When a recipe calls for chopped cooked chicken, it can be difficult to judge how much chicken to purchase. As a guideline, 2 whole chicken breasts (about 10 ounces each) will yield about 2 cups of chopped cooked chicken; 1 broiling/frying chicken (about 3 pounds) will yield about 2½ cups chopped cooked chicken.

Tortilla Soup

Thai Chicken Broccoli Salad

4 ounces uncooked linguine
   Nonstick cooking spray
½ pound boneless skinless chicken breasts, cut into bite-size pieces
2 cups broccoli florets
2 tablespoons cold water
⅔ cup chopped red bell pepper
6 green onions, sliced diagonally into 1-inch pieces
¼ cup creamy peanut butter
2 tablespoons hot water
2 tablespoons soy sauce
2 teaspoons dark sesame oil
½ teaspoon red pepper flakes
⅛ teaspoon garlic powder
¼ cup unsalted peanuts, chopped

1. Cook pasta according to package directions. Drain; set aside.

2. Spray large nonstick skillet with cooking spray; heat over medium-high heat. Add chicken; stir-fry 5 minutes or until chicken is cooked through. Transfer chicken to large bowl.

3. Add broccoli and cold water to skillet. Cook, covered, 2 minutes. Uncover; cook and stir 2 minutes or until broccoli is crisp-tender. Transfer broccoli to bowl with chicken. Add pasta, bell pepper and green onions; stir to combine.

4. Combine peanut butter, hot water, soy sauce, oil, red pepper flakes and garlic powder in small bowl until well blended. Drizzle over pasta mixture; toss to coat. Top with peanuts before serving.

Makes 4 servings

Nancy's Chicken Noodle Soup

1 can (about 48 ounces) chicken broth
2 boneless skinless chicken breasts, cut into bite-size pieces
4 cups water
⅔ cup diced onion
⅔ cup diced celery
⅔ cup diced carrots
⅔ cup sliced mushrooms
½ cup frozen peas
4 chicken bouillon cubes
2 tablespoons butter
1 tablespoon dried parsley flakes
1 teaspoon salt
1 teaspoon ground cumin
1 teaspoon dried marjoram
1 teaspoon black pepper
2 cups cooked egg noodles

Slow Cooker Directions

1. Combine all ingredients except noodles in 5-quart slow cooker.

2. Cover; cook on LOW 5 to 7 hours or on HIGH 3 to 4 hours. Stir in noodles 30 minutes before serving. *Makes 4 servings*

note

For easier preparation, cut up ingredients for the slow cooker the night before. Wrap and store meats and vegetables separately in the refrigerator. Make sure to cut the ingredients into uniform pieces so that everything cooks evenly.

Chicken Tortellini Soup

6 cups chicken broth

1 package (9 ounces) refrigerated cheese and spinach tortellini or three-cheese tortellini

1 package (about 6 ounces) refrigerated fully cooked chicken breast strips, cut into bite-size pieces

2 cups coarsely chopped baby spinach

4 to 6 tablespoons grated Parmesan cheese

1 tablespoon chopped fresh chives *or* 2 tablespoons sliced green onion

1. Bring broth to a boil in large saucepan over high heat; add tortellini. Reduce heat to medium; cook 5 minutes. Stir in chicken and spinach.

2. Reduce heat to low; cook 3 minutes or until chicken is heated through. Sprinkle with Parmesan cheese and chives.

Makes 4 servings

note

Baby spinach is often sold already bagged and washed. Before purchasing, inspect the package closely to make sure there are no wet spots or brown edges on individual leaves, and that the leaves are not sticking together.

Chicken Tortellini Soup

Hearty Chicken Chili

1 medium onion, finely chopped
1 small jalapeño pepper,* minced
1 clove garlic, minced
1½ teaspoons chili powder
¾ teaspoon salt
½ teaspoon ground cumin
½ teaspoon dried oregano
½ teaspoon black pepper
1½ pounds boneless skinless chicken thighs, cut into 1-inch pieces
2 cans (about 15 ounces each) hominy, rinsed and drained
1 can (about 15 ounces) pinto beans, rinsed and drained
1 cup chicken broth
1 tablespoon all-purpose flour (optional)
Chopped fresh parsley or fresh cilantro (optional)

Jalapeño peppers can sting and irritate the skin, so wear rubber gloves when handling peppers and do not touch your eyes.

Slow Cooker Directions

1. Combine onion, jalapeño, garlic, chili powder, salt, cumin, oregano and pepper in slow cooker.

2. Add chicken, hominy, beans and broth. Stir well to combine. Cover; cook on LOW 7 hours.

3. If thicker gravy is desired, combine 1 tablespoon flour and 3 tablespoons cooking liquid in small bowl. Add to slow cooker. Cover; cook on HIGH 10 minutes or until thickened. Garnish with parsley. *Makes 6 servings*

Prep Time: 15 minutes
Cook Time: 7 hours (LOW), plus 10 minutes (HIGH)

Hearty Chicken Chili

Chicken and Pasta Salad with Kalamata Olives

4 ounces uncooked multigrain rotini
2 cups diced cooked chicken
½ cup chopped roasted red bell peppers
12 pitted kalamata olives, halved
1½ tablespoons olive oil
1 tablespoon dried basil
1 tablespoon cider vinegar
1 to 2 cloves garlic, minced
¼ teaspoon salt

1. Cook rotini according to package directions. Drain and cool.

2. Combine chicken, peppers, olives, oil, basil, vinegar, garlic and salt in medium bowl.

3. Add cooled pasta to chicken mixture; toss gently. Divide equally among 4 plates. *Makes 4 servings*

note

Kalamata olives are from Greece. They are almond-shaped with a dark purplish-black color. They are soaked in a wine vinegar marinade and have a rich, fruity flavor.

Chicken and Pasta Salad with Kalamata Olives

family favorites

Chicken Cacciatore

¼ cup vegetable oil
2½ to 3 pounds chicken tenders, cut into bite-size pieces
1 can (28 ounces) crushed Italian-style tomatoes
2 cans (8 ounces each) Italian-style tomato sauce
1 medium onion, chopped
1 can (4 ounces) sliced mushrooms, drained
2 cloves garlic, minced
1 teaspoon salt
1 teaspoon dried oregano
½ teaspoon dried thyme
½ teaspoon black pepper
Hot cooked spaghetti

Slow Cooker Directions

1. Heat oil in large skillet over medium-low heat. Brown chicken on all sides. Drain excess fat.

2. Transfer chicken to slow cooker. Add remaining ingredients except spaghetti. Cover; cook on LOW 6 to 8 hours. Serve over spaghetti. *Makes 6 to 8 servings*

Chicken and Herb Stew

½ cup all-purpose flour
½ teaspoon salt
¼ teaspoon black pepper
¼ teaspoon paprika
4 chicken drumsticks
4 chicken thighs
2 tablespoons olive oil
12 ounces new potatoes, quartered
2 medium carrots, quartered lengthwise and cut into 3-inch pieces
1 green bell pepper, cut into thin strips
¾ cup chopped onion
2 medium cloves garlic, minced
1¾ cups water
¼ cup dry white wine
2 chicken bouillon cubes
1 tablespoon chopped fresh oregano
1 teaspoon chopped fresh rosemary leaves
2 tablespoons chopped fresh parsley (optional)

1. Combine flour, salt, black pepper and paprika in shallow dish. Stir until well blended. Coat chicken pieces with flour mixture; shake off excess.

2. Heat oil in large skillet over medium-high heat; add chicken. Brown evenly on both sides, turning frequently, about 8 minutes. Remove from skillet; set aside.

3. Add potatoes, carrots, bell pepper, onion and garlic to skillet. Cook and stir 5 minutes or until vegetables are lightly browned. Add water, wine and bouillon. Cook and stir, scraping up browned bits from bottom of skillet. Add oregano and rosemary.

4. Arrange chicken pieces on top of vegetable mixture, turning several times to coat. Cover tightly and simmer 45 to 50 minutes or until chicken is cooked through (165°F), turning occasionally. Garnish with parsley. *Makes 4 servings*

Chicken and Herb Stew

Honey-Roasted Chicken and Butternut Squash

Nonstick cooking spray
1 pound (16 ounces) fresh butternut squash chunks
Salt and black pepper
6 bone-in chicken thighs
1 tablespoon honey

1. Preheat oven to 375°F. Spray baking sheet and wire rack with cooking spray.

2. Spread squash chunks on baking sheet. Season with salt and pepper; toss to coat.

3. Place wire rack on top of squash; place chicken on rack. Season with salt and pepper.

4. Bake 25 minutes. Carefully lift rack and stir squash; brush honey over chicken pieces. Bake 20 minutes or until chicken is cooked through (165°F). *Makes 4 to 6 servings*

Cheesy Chicken & Broccoli Fettuccine

1 to 2 tablespoons olive oil
1 pound boneless skinless chicken breasts, cut into 1-inch pieces
2 boxes (10 ounces each) frozen broccoli with cheese sauce, defrosted
1 package (12 ounces) fresh fettuccine, cooked and drained
Salt and black pepper

1. Heat oil in large skillet over medium-high heat. Add chicken; cook and stir about 10 minutes or until cooked through.

2. Stir in broccoli and cheese sauce; heat until crisp-tender.

3. Add fettuccine; stir to coat with cheese mixture. Season with salt and pepper. *Makes 8 servings*

Honey-Roasted Chicken and Butternut Squash

Spanish Chicken and Rice

- 1 tablespoon olive oil
- 1 pound boneless skinless chicken breasts, diced
- 1 medium onion, chopped
- 1 medium red bell pepper, chopped
- 1 cup chicken broth
- 1 can (15 ounces) Spanish-style diced tomatoes, undrained
- 1 cup frozen peas
- 1 teaspoon garlic powder
- 1 teaspoon turmeric (optional)
- 2 cups MINUTE® White Rice, uncooked

Heat oil in large skillet over medium-high heat. Cook chicken, onion and bell pepper until chicken is browned, stirring occasionally. Add broth, tomatoes, peas, garlic powder and turmeric, if desired; bring to a boil. Stir in rice. Reduce heat to low; cover. Cook 5 minutes or until rice is tender.

Makes 4 servings

Tip: To make Easy Paella with Shrimp, add ½ pound peeled and deveined medium shrimp at the same time as the broth.

note

Turmeric is a spice that is related to ginger. It has an exotic fragrance and lends flavor and a deep yellow color to dishes. It is an essential component of curry powder and is used often in Indian and Middle Eastern cooking. Use turmeric sparingly—a little goes a long way.

Spanish Chicken and Rice

Chicken Fingers with Dijonaise Dipping Sauce

Dijonaise Sauce

> 3 tablespoons mayonnaise
>
> 2 tablespoons honey Dijon mustard
>
> 1 tablespoon lemon juice

Chicken Fingers

> ¾ cup CREAM OF WHEAT® Hot Cereal (Instant, 1-minute, 2½-minute or 10-minute cook time), uncooked
>
> ¾ cup grated Parmesan cheese
>
> ¾ teaspoon ground paprika
>
> ¼ cup milk
>
> 2 eggs
>
> 4 boneless skinless chicken breasts (1 pound)
>
> Nonstick cooking spray

1. Combine all sauce ingredients in small bowl; set aside until ready to use.

2. Preheat oven to 450°F. Coat baking sheet with nonstick cooking spray. Combine Cream of Wheat, cheese and paprika in shallow bowl; set aside. Combine milk and eggs in second shallow bowl; set aside.

3. Flatten chicken breasts slightly to uniform thickness. Cut into strips. Dip each strip into Cream of Wheat mixture, coating evenly. Dip into egg mixture, coating evenly. Dip into Cream of Wheat mixture again, coating evenly. Place strips on prepared baking sheet. Lightly coat strips with cooking spray. Bake 6 minutes; turn over strips and bake 6 minutes longer. Serve with Dijonaise sauce or your favorite dipping sauce. *Makes 4 servings*

Tip: To create a one-dish dinner, serve chicken fingers over a crunchy fresh salad.

Prep Time: 10 minutes
Start to Finish Time: 25 minutes

Chicken Fingers with Dijonaise Dipping Sauce

Oven-Fried Bbq Glazed Chicken

1 cup all-purpose flour
1 tablespoon LAWRY'S® Seasoned Salt
1 teaspoon LAWRY'S® Garlic Salt
1 teaspoon LAWRY'S® Seasoned Pepper
3 pounds chicken legs and/or bone-in chicken thighs
1 cup milk
1 cup barbecue sauce

1. Preheat oven to 425°F. Spray jelly roll pan with nonstick cooking spray; set aside.

2. In large resealable plastic bag, combine flour, LAWRY'S® Seasoned Salt, Garlic Salt and Seasoned Pepper. Dip chicken in milk, then add to bag; shake to coat. On prepared pan, arrange chicken skin-side up.

3. Bake, turning once, 35 minutes. Generously coat with barbecue sauce. Bake an additional 5 minutes or until chicken is thoroughly cooked. *Makes 8 servings*

Prep Time: 10 minutes
Cook Time: 40 minutes

Lemony Greek Chicken

1 whole chicken (about 3 to 4 pounds), cut up
1 tablespoon olive oil
2 teaspoons Greek seasoning
1 teaspoon salt
1 teaspoon black pepper
  Juice of 1 lemon

1. Preheat oven to 400°F. Brush chicken with oil. Arrange in 2 large baking dishes, bone side down. Combine Greek seasoning, salt and pepper in small bowl; sprinkle half over chicken. Bake 30 minutes.

2. Turn chicken over. Sprinkle with remaining seasoning mixture and lemon juice. Bake 30 minutes or until chicken is cooked through (165°F). *Makes 4 to 6 servings*

Oven-Fried Bbq Glazed Chicken

Easy Chicken Alfredo

1½ pounds boneless skinless chicken breasts, cut into ½-inch pieces
1 medium onion, chopped
1 tablespoon dried chives
1 tablespoon dried basil
1 tablespoon extra-virgin olive oil
1 teaspoon lemon pepper
¼ teaspoon ground ginger
½ pound broccoli, coarsely chopped
1 red bell pepper, chopped
1 can (8 ounces) sliced water chestnuts, drained
1 cup baby carrots
3 cloves garlic, minced
1 jar (16 ounces) Alfredo sauce
1 package (8 ounces) wide egg noodles, cooked and drained

Slow Cooker Directions

1. Combine chicken, onion, chives, basil, oil, lemon pepper and ginger in slow cooker; mix well. Add broccoli, bell pepper, water chestnuts, carrots and garlic; mix well.

2. Cover; cook on LOW 8 hours or on HIGH 4 hours.

3. Add Alfredo sauce. Cover; cook on HIGH 30 minutes or until heated through. Serve over hot cooked egg noodles.

Makes 6 servings

note

Dairy products, such as the Alfredo sauce used in this recipe, should be added at the end of the cooking time because they will curdle if cooked in the slow cooker for a long time.

Chicken Pesto Pizza

Cornmeal
1 loaf (1 pound) frozen bread dough, thawed
Nonstick cooking spray
8 ounces chicken tenders, cut into ½-inch pieces
½ red onion, thinly sliced
¼ cup pesto
2 large plum tomatoes, seeded and diced
1 cup (4 ounces) shredded pizza cheese blend or mozzarella cheese

1. Preheat oven to 375°F. Sprinkle baking sheet with cornmeal. Roll out bread dough on floured surface to 14×8-inch rectangle. Transfer to prepared baking sheet. Cover loosely with plastic wrap; let rise 20 to 30 minutes.

2. Meanwhile, spray large skillet with cooking spray. Add chicken; cook and stir over medium heat 2 minutes. Add onion and pesto; cook and stir 3 to 4 minutes or until chicken is cooked through. Stir in tomatoes; let cool slightly.

3. Spread chicken mixture evenly over dough to within 1 inch of edges. Sprinkle with cheese.

4. Bake on bottom rack of oven about 20 minutes or until crust is golden brown. Cut into squares. *Makes 4 servings*

note

From the Italian word meaning pounded, pesto is a green uncooked sauce from Italy made from fresh basil, garlic, pine nuts, Parmesan cheese and olive oil. The ingredients are mashed together, traditionally in a mortar and pestle, but today, more likely in a food processor. Variations of the classic pesto can be found with various herbs substituted for the traditional basil.

Sweet and Sour Chicken

¼ cup chicken broth
2 tablespoons soy sauce
2 tablespoons hoisin sauce
1 tablespoon cider vinegar
1 tablespoon tomato paste
2 teaspoons packed brown sugar
1 clove garlic, minced
¼ teaspoon black pepper
1 pound boneless skinless chicken thighs, cut into 1-inch pieces
2 teaspoons cornstarch
2 tablespoons minced chives
   Hot cooked rice

Slow Cooker Directions

1. Combine broth, soy sauce, hoisin sauce, cider vinegar, tomato paste, brown sugar, garlic and pepper in slow cooker. Stir well.

2. Add chicken and stir. Cover; cook on LOW 2½ to 3½ hours.

3. Remove chicken with slotted spoon; keep warm. Combine cornstarch and 2 tablespoons cooking liquid in a cup. Add to slow cooker. Stir in chives. *Turn slow cooker to HIGH.* Stir 2 minutes or until sauce is slightly thickened. Serve chicken and sauce over rice.

Makes 4 servings

Prep Time: 10 minutes
Cook Time: 2½ to 3½ hours

Sweet and Sour Chicken

Crispy Buttermilk Fried Chicken

2 cups buttermilk
1 tablespoon hot pepper sauce
3 pounds bone-in chicken pieces
2 cups all-purpose flour
2 teaspoons salt
2 teaspoons poultry seasoning
1 teaspoon garlic salt
1 teaspoon paprika
1 teaspoon ground red pepper
1 teaspoon black pepper
1 cup vegetable oil

1. Combine buttermilk and hot pepper sauce in large resealable food storage bag. Add chicken; seal bag. Turn to coat; refrigerate 2 hours or up to 24 hours.

2. Combine flour, salt, poultry seasoning, garlic salt, paprika, red pepper and black pepper in another large food storage bag or shallow baking dish; blend well. Working in batches, remove chicken from buttermilk; shake off excess. Add to flour mixture; shake to coat.

3. Heat oil over medium heat in heavy deep skillet to 350°F. Fry chicken in batches 30 minutes or until cooked through (165°F), turning occasionally to brown all sides. (Allow oil to return to temperature between batches.)

4. Drain on paper towels. Serve immediately.   *Makes 4 servings*

Prep Time: 15 minutes
Cook Time: 30 minutes
Marinating Time: 2 to 24 hours

Crispy Buttermilk Fried Chicken

Creamy Chicken and Spinach Lasagna

- 1¼ cups shredded Swiss or mozzarella cheese, divided
- 1 cup ricotta cheese
- 1 teaspoon dried oregano
- ¼ teaspoon red pepper flakes
- 1 container (10 ounces) refrigerated Alfredo-style pasta sauce
- ⅓ cup water
- 4 no-boil lasagna noodles
- 1 package (10 ounces) frozen chopped spinach, thawed and squeezed dry
- ¼ cup grated Parmesan cheese
- 1½ cups diced cooked chicken
- Red pepper flakes (optional)

Slow Cooker Directions

1. Combine 1 cup Swiss cheese, ricotta, oregano and pepper flakes in small bowl; set aside. Blend Alfredo sauce with water in medium bowl; set aside.

2. Coat slow cooker with nonstick cooking spray. Break 2 lasagna noodles in half and place on bottom. Spread half of ricotta mixture over noodles. Top with half of spinach. Arrange half of chicken and half of Parmesan over spinach. Pour half of Alfredo mixture over top. Repeat layers.

3. Cover; cook on LOW 3 hours. Sprinkle remaining ¼ cup Swiss cheese on top. Cover and let stand 5 minutes or until cheese is melted. Cut into squares or wedges. Garnish with pepper flakes.

Makes 4 servings

Prep Time: 20 minutes
Cook Time: 3 hours (LOW)

Pineapple Teriyaki Chicken Kabobs

1 can (20 ounce) DOLE® Pineapple Chunks
¾ cup LAWRY'S® Teriyaki Marinade with Pineapple Juice
1 teaspoon Dijon-style mustard
4 (1½- to 1¾-pound) boneless, skinless chicken breasts
  cut into 1-inch pieces
2 red or green bell peppers, cut into 1½-inch pieces
1 zucchini cut into ½-inch-thick slices
12 wooden skewers (12 inches long) soaked in water

- Drain pineapple; reserve 2 tablespoons juice.

- Combine pineapple juice, teriyaki marinade and mustard. Set aside ¼ cup for grilling. Pour remaining marinade into sealable plastic bag; add chicken pieces, bell peppers and zucchini. Refrigerate and marinate for 30 minutes.

- Remove chicken and vegetables from plastic bag and discard marinade.

- Thread bell pepper, pineapple chunks, chicken and zucchini onto skewers. Brush with reserved marinade.

- Grill or broil 10 to 15 minutes, turning and brushing occasionally with teriyaki marinade, or until chicken is no longer pink. Discard any remaining marinade. *Makes 4 servings*

Prep Time: 15 minutes
Grill Time: 15 minutes

note

Skewers are threaded with small chunks or strips of meat, poultry, vegetables and sometimes fruit to make kabobs for grilling. Metal skewers are best for heavier foods like chunks of meat. Long, thin wooden skewers work well for small pieces of meat, vegetables and fruits. Soak wooden skewers in water for about 30 minutes before using to prevent burning.

Nice 'n' Easy Italian Chicken

4 boneless skinless chicken breasts (about 1 pound)
8 ounces mushrooms, sliced
1 medium green bell pepper, chopped (optional)
1 medium zucchini, diced
1 medium onion, chopped
1 jar (26 ounces) pasta sauce
Hot cooked pasta

Slow Cooker Directions

Combine all ingredients except pasta in slow cooker. Cover; cook on LOW 6 to 8 hours or until chicken is tender. Serve over pasta.

Makes 4 servings

Roast Chicken with Peppers

1 chicken (3 to 3½ pounds), cut into pieces
3 tablespoons olive oil, divided
1 tablespoon plus 1½ teaspoons chopped fresh rosemary leaves *or* 1½ teaspoons dried rosemary
1 tablespoon fresh lemon juice
1¼ teaspoons salt, divided
¾ teaspoon black pepper, divided
3 bell peppers (red, yellow and/or green)
1 medium onion

1. Preheat oven to 375°F. Place chicken in shallow roasting pan.

2. Combine 2 tablespoons oil, rosemary and lemon juice in small bowl; brush over chicken. Sprinkle 1 teaspoon salt and ½ teaspoon black pepper over chicken. Roast 15 minutes.

3. Cut bell peppers lengthwise into ½-inch-thick strips. Cut onion into thin wedges. Toss vegetables with remaining 1 tablespoon oil, ¼ teaspoon salt and ¼ teaspoon pepper in medium bowl. Spoon vegetables around chicken; roast about 40 minutes or until vegetables are tender and chicken is cooked through (165°F). Serve chicken with vegetables and pan juices. *Makes 6 servings*

Nice 'n' Easy Italian Chicken

Acknowledgments

The publisher would like to thank the companies and organizations listed below for the use of their recipes in this publication.

Cream of Wheat® Cereal

Dole Food Company, Inc.

The Golden Grain Company®

Ortega®, A Division of B&G Foods, Inc.

Reckitt Benckiser Inc.

Riviana Foods Inc.

Unilever

VOLUME MEASUREMENTS (dry)

1/8 teaspoon = 0.5 mL
1/4 teaspoon = 1 mL
1/2 teaspoon = 2 mL
3/4 teaspoon = 4 mL
1 teaspoon = 5 mL
1 tablespoon = 15 mL
2 tablespoons = 30 mL
1/4 cup = 60 mL
1/3 cup = 75 mL
1/2 cup = 125 mL
2/3 cup = 150 mL
3/4 cup = 175 mL
1 cup = 250 mL
2 cups = 1 pint = 500 mL
3 cups = 750 mL
4 cups = 1 quart = 1 L

VOLUME MEASUREMENTS (fluid)

1 fluid ounce (2 tablespoons) = 30 mL
4 fluid ounces (1/2 cup) = 125 mL
8 fluid ounces (1 cup) = 250 mL
12 fluid ounces (1 1/2 cups) = 375 mL
16 fluid ounces (2 cups) = 500 mL

WEIGHTS (mass)

1/2 ounce = 15 g
1 ounce = 30 g
3 ounces = 90 g
4 ounces = 120 g
8 ounces = 225 g
10 ounces = 285 g
12 ounces = 360 g
16 ounces = 1 pound = 450 g

DIMENSIONS

1/16 inch = 2 mm
1/8 inch = 3 mm
1/4 inch = 6 mm
1/2 inch = 1.5 cm
3/4 inch = 2 cm
1 inch = 2.5 cm

OVEN TEMPERATURES

250°F = 120°C
275°F = 140°C
300°F = 150°C
325°F = 160°C
350°F = 180°C
375°F = 190°C
400°F = 200°C
425°F = 220°C
450°F = 230°C

BAKING PAN SIZES

Utensil	Size in Inches/Quarts	Metric Volume	Size in Centimeters
Baking or Cake Pan (square or rectangular)	8×8×2	2 L	20×20×5
	9×9×2	2.5 L	23×23×5
	12×8×2	3 L	30×20×5
	13×9×2	3.5 L	33×23×5
Loaf Pan	8×4×3	1.5 L	20×10×7
	9×5×3	2 L	23×13×7
Round Layer Cake Pan	8×1½	1.2 L	20×4
	9×1½	1.5 L	23×4
Pie Plate	8×1¼	750 mL	20×3
	9×1¼	1 L	23×3
Baking Dish or Casserole	1 quart	1 L	—
	1½ quart	1.5 L	—
	2 quart	2 L	—